enrich-e-matics
3ʳᵈ EDITION

BOOK 6

Anne Joshua

MA, Dip Ed (Syd); MSc (Oxon)

T0363986

enrich-e-matics
3rd EDITION

Dear Teachers, Students and Parents,

Thank you for purchasing *Enrich-e-matics 3rd Edition*. This is the sixth of a series of six books designed to develop and enrich students' problem-solving skills. *Enrich-e-matics 3rd Edition* deepens students' mathematical concepts and encourages flexibility of thinking along with a willingness to tackle challenging and fascinating problems. The series was originally designed to cater for the mathematically able student but was also found to be a useful tool for all schools wishing to strengthen their students' mathematical understanding.

What is different about *Enrich-e-matics 3rd Edition*?

Enrich-e-matics 3rd Edition is much more than a collection of puzzles and difficult problems. The exercises are *graded*. Concepts and strategies are developed throughout the series to provide for a systematic development of problem-solving and mathematical ability.

The exercises and activities have been grouped into mathematics strands—**Number, Patterns & Algebra, Chance & Data, Measurement, Space** and **Working Mathematically**—with hundreds of new problems added. This allows students and teachers to work systematically through a number of similar problems focusing on one area of mathematics. It also allows flexibility of programming so that material from different strands can be integrated. The strand is indicated on each page by an icon. Themes are introduced and developed throughout the series. The answers for all problems are included in a removable section at the back of the book.

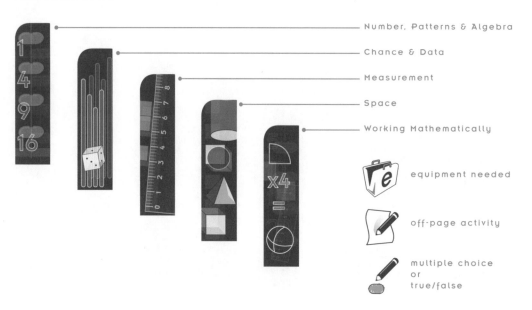

Number, Patterns & Algebra

Chance & Data

Measurement

Space

Working Mathematically

equipment needed

off-page activity

multiple choice or true/false

In *Enrich-e-matics 3rd Edition* explanations and worked examples are highlighted. The space for students to write answers and show their working has been maximised in this new edition. An icon has been used to show where students may need extra paper or equipment to complete the problems. Multiple choice and true/false questions use shaded bubbles similar to those used in state and national test papers.

Enrich-e-matics 3rd Edition is designed to meet the needs of students by:

- providing challenging problems for enrichment and extension
- reinforcing concepts and skills
- developing problem-solving strategies and extending mathematical insight, ability and logical thought
- providing opportunities to experience the joy of problem solving
- providing a ready source of challenging problems to prepare students for mathematics competitions

all of which build the foundation for excellence in mathematics.

The *Enrich-e-matics* series may be used to supplement and be integrated into the school's mathematics program.

The *Enrich-e-matics 3rd Edition Teacher's Book* is available to assist teachers implement the enrichment program in their school. It is a most valuable resource containing teaching suggestions, worked solutions and reproducible material. Most importantly it also contains highly valued screening tests that help to identify mathematical ability.

Who can use this book?

Enrich-e-matics 3rd Edition Book 6 may be used by:

- a group of able students working together in class
- classes in selective schools or maths extension groups
- an individual student at home.

The books have been extensively trialled, over several years, with students aged 6 to 15 in schools and at various camps for gifted and talented students. *Enrich-e-matics 3rd Edition Book 6* is aimed at 11 to 13 year olds.

To gain the maximum advantage from the series encourage students to discuss their solutions in small groups, with their teacher or with parents at home. This discussion of ideas enhances learning.

I hope that you will find *Enrich-e-matics 3rd Edition* enjoyable and challenging, and that you remain curious and motivated mathematics students.

Anne Joshua

Contents

ANSWERS
lift-out at the back of book

Missing numbers

Each of the four shapes  represents a mathematical operation (e.g. + 7 or × 5).

Find the rule governing each shape, fill these in and work out what the missing numbers are.

		RULE		RULE		RULE		RULE	

1   5 → □ → 10 → ○ → 40 → △ → 32 → ◇ → 16

2   9 → □ → 14 → ○ → 56 → △ → 48 → ◇ → 24

3   10 → □ → ___ → ○ → ___ → △ → ___ → ◇ → 26

4   11 → □ → ___ → ○ → ___ → △ → ___ → ◇ → ___

5   ___ → □ → 12 → ○ → ___ → △ → ___ → ◇ → ___

6   ___ → □ → ___ → ○ → 44 → △ → ___ → ◇ → ___

7   ___ → □ → ___ → ○ → ___ → △ → 24 → ◇ → ___

8   ___ → □ → ___ → ○ → ___ → △ → 28 → ◇ → ___

9   ___ → □ → ___ → ○ → ___ → △ → ___ → ◇ → 10

10   ___ → □ → ___ → ○ → ___ → △ → ___ → ◇ → 36

11   ___ → □ → ___ → ○ → ___ → △ → ___ → ◇ → 6

12   ___ → □ → ___ → ○ → ___ → △ → ___ → ◇ → 7

13   ___ → □ → ___ → ○ → ___ → △ → ___ → ◇ → $7\frac{1}{2}$

14   ___ → □ → ___ → ○ → ___ → △ → ___ → ◇ → $6\frac{1}{2}$

Secret rules

In each exercise there is a secret rule connecting the numbers in the first row with those in the second row. First discover the rule and then find the missing numbers.

RULE

1

4	7	3	2	10	8	5	11	13	
5	11	3	1						

2

7	10	5	4	3	2	9	11	8	
50	101	26	17						

3

4	5	8	2	7	10	3	9	11	
22	27	42	12						

4

8	3	2	7	4	10	5	6	12	
22	7	4	19						

5

8	3	10	7	4	2	5	1	6	
21	11	25	19						

6

4	2	9	6	5	3	8	7	10	
9	1	64	25						

7

2	5	7	3	8	6	4	11	1	
17	44	62	26						

8

4	7	8	6	5	3	2	10	9	
12	18	20	16						

9

6	3	9	5	4	1	2	10	7	
15	6	24	12						

10

6	3	9	5	4	1	2	10	12	
30	6	72	20						

Square puzzles

Can you find the values of the letters A, B, C, D and E in these squares? The sum of each row and column is given, and only the numbers 1, 2, 3, 4 and 5 are used. One letter value is given for each square.

1

E	D	A	10
B	A	C	10
D	C	B	6

8 8 10

A	B	C	D	E
__	__	__	__	4

4			10
			10
			6

8 8 10

2

B	C	D	6
E	A	C	10
C	B	E	8

8 9 7

A	B	C	D	E
5	__	__	__	__

			6
	5		10
			8

8 9 7

3

C	A	D	8
A	B	E	9
D	C	C	11

8 10 10

A	B	C	D	E
__	__	__	__	4

			8
		4	9
			11

8 10 10

4

A	B	C	11
D	E	A	6
B	C	D	12

10 10 9

A	B	C	D	E
__	__	__	__	1

			11
	1		6
			12

10 10 9

5

E	B	D	10
D	A	C	10
C	E	B	6

9 9 8

A	B	C	D	E
4	__	__	__	__

			10
	4		10
			6

9 9 8

Find three numbers

In each group of equations I am thinking of three numbers $\square$, $\triangle$ and $\bigcirc$. You can find my three numbers by using the clues given.

1
$\bigcirc + \square = 14$

$\bigcirc - \square = 4$

$\bigcirc + 1 = \triangle$

$\square + \square = \triangle$

2
$\triangle + \square = 19$

$\triangle - \square = 3$

$\bigcirc + \triangle = \square + 4$

$\bigcirc + \bigcirc + 6 = \square$

3
$\square + \square = \triangle$

$\triangle - \square = 6$

$\bigcirc + \bigcirc = \square + \square + \square$

$\bigcirc + \square = \triangle + 3$

4
$\triangle + \triangle + \triangle = \square$

$\square + \triangle = 16$

$\triangle + \triangle + = \bigcirc$

$\bigcirc + \bigcirc + \bigcirc = \square + \square$

5
$\triangle + \triangle + \triangle = \bigcirc + \bigcirc$

$\triangle + \bigcirc = 10$

$\square \div \bigcirc = \triangle$

6
$\triangle - \bigcirc = \bigcirc + 2$

$\triangle + \bigcirc = 11$

$\square \div \bigcirc = \triangle$

7
$\bigcirc - \triangle = 2$

$\bigcirc + \triangle = 10$

$\bigcirc \times \bigcirc = \square$

$\square \div \triangle = 9$

8
$\bigcirc + \bigcirc + 1 = \triangle$

$\triangle + \bigcirc = 13$

$\triangle - \bigcirc = 5$

$\square \div \triangle = \bigcirc$

9
$\triangle \times \square = \bigcirc$

$\triangle - \square = 1$

$\triangle \times \triangle = \bigcirc + 5$

$\bigcirc - \triangle = 15$

10
$\triangle \times \triangle \times \triangle = \square$

$\bigcirc - \triangle = 5$

$\bigcirc \times \triangle = \square - \triangle$

$\square = \bigcirc + \bigcirc + \bigcirc + \triangle$

What's my pattern?

If you were asked to complete the pattern: 1, 2, 4, ... you could do it in a number of ways.

Sequence	Pattern
1, 2, 4, 8, 16, 32	Times 2
1, 2, 4, 7, 11, 16 1 2 3 4 5	Add 1, add 2, add 3 ..., or differences increasing by 1
1, 2, 4, 5, 7, 8 1 2 1 2 1	Differences 1 and 2, or 2 patterns: 1, 4, 7 … and 2, 5, 8 …
1, 2, 4 , 8, 10, 20	Times 2, add 2
1, 2, 4, 5, 10, 11	Add 1, times 2

Complete the patterns below in as many different ways as you can, writing down the next three terms for each one.

1 1, 3, 9 _____ , _____ , _____   or   _____ , _____ , _____   or   _____ , _____ , _____

2 1, 4, 5 _____ , _____ , _____   _____ , _____ , _____   _____ , _____ , _____

3 1, 3, 6 _____ , _____ , _____   _____ , _____ , _____   _____ , _____ , _____

4 2, 3, 5 _____ , _____ , _____   _____ , _____ , _____   _____ , _____ , _____

5 1, 1, 2 _____ , _____ , _____   _____ , _____ , _____   _____ , _____ , _____

6 1, 4, 9 _____ , _____ , _____   _____ , _____ , _____   _____ , _____ , _____

7 2, 4, 6 _____ , _____ , _____   _____ , _____ , _____   _____ , _____ , _____

8 3, 4, 6 _____ , _____ , _____   _____ , _____ , _____   _____ , _____ , _____

9 $\frac{1}{2}$, 1, $1\frac{1}{2}$ _____ , _____ , _____   _____ , _____ , _____   _____ , _____ , _____

10 0, 1, 10 _____ , _____ , _____   _____ , _____ , _____   _____ , _____ , _____

11 3, 6, 12 _____ , _____ , _____   _____ , _____ , _____   _____ , _____ , _____

12 1, 5, 25 _____ , _____ , _____   _____ , _____ , _____   _____ , _____ , _____

Magic squares

1 Complete these squares so that in each one every row, column and diagonal has the same sum.

a

$2\frac{1}{2}$		
5	3	
		$3\frac{1}{2}$

b

		$\frac{1}{4}$
		2
$1\frac{3}{4}$		$\frac{3}{4}$

c

$\frac{1}{3}$		
	$1\frac{1}{3}$	$\frac{2}{3}$
		$2\frac{1}{3}$

d

		$1\frac{4}{5}$
2	$1\frac{1}{5}$	
$\frac{3}{5}$		

e

$1\frac{1}{2}$	$1\frac{1}{4}$	$2\frac{1}{2}$
	$1\frac{3}{4}$	

f

		0·2
	0·5	
0·8	0·3	

g

0·7		
	0·6	
0·9		0·5

h

	0·7	
	0·9	0·5
	1·1	1

2 What are my two numbers if:

a the sum of the two numbers is 5·2 and their difference is 0·4? _____ _____

b the sum of the two numbers is 7·5 and their difference is 0·5? _____ _____

c the sum of the two numbers is 7·5 and their difference is 0·1? _____ _____

d the sum of the two numbers is 7·5 and their difference is 1·0? _____ _____

e the sum of the two numbers is 4·5 and their product is 5? _____ _____

f the sum of the two numbers is 6·5 and their product is 9? _____ _____

g the sum of the two numbers is 6·5 and their product is 5·5? _____ _____

h the sum of the two numbers is 6·5 and their product is 0·64? _____ _____

i the sum of the two numbers is 4·2 and their product is 4·4? _____ _____

j the sum of the two numbers is 4·2 and their product is 0·8? _____ _____

Decimal challenges

Colour in the bubble next to the answer.

1 Four of the following are equal. Which is different?

A ◯ 0·02   B ◯ $\frac{1}{50}$ C ◯ 5% of 1   D ◯ 20 thousandths   E ◯ 1% of 2

2 If Sam scored 19 out of 20 in a game, which of the following is not his score?

A ◯ $\frac{95}{100}$ B ◯ 0·19   C ◯ $\frac{19}{20}$ D ◯ 95%   E ◯ 0·95

3 Which is closest to 0·7?

A ◯ 67%   B ◯ 75%   C ◯ 0·6   D ◯ 0·74   E ◯ 0·629

4 David recorded the lowest temperatures over five days in winter. Which temperature was the coldest?

A ◯ 10·3°C   B ◯ 10·33°C   C ◯ 10·033°C   D ◯ 10·03°C   E ◯ 10·30°C

5 Which is the smallest of the following numbers?

A ◯ 89·9   B ◯ 89·09   C ◯ 89·90   D ◯ 89·99   E ◯ 89·009

6 $8\frac{1}{2}$% as a decimal is:

A ◯ 0·0805   B ◯ 0·85   C ◯ 8·5   D ◯ 0·0085   E ◯ 0·085

7 The simplest form of expressing 0·625 as a fraction is:

A ◯ $\frac{625}{1000}$ B ◯ $\frac{125}{200}$ C ◯ $\frac{5}{8}$ D ◯ $\frac{3}{4}$ E ◯ $6\frac{1}{4}$

8 Which of the following numbers remains unchanged in value when the zero is removed?

A ◯ 2·490   B ◯ 350   C ◯ 6·04   D ◯ 20·73   E ◯ 108·7

9 Which of the following decimal expressions is equivalent to the sum of: $\frac{2}{10}$ and $\frac{6}{1000}$?

A ◯ 0·26   B ◯ 0·206   C ◯ 0·0206   D ◯ 0·2006   E ◯ 0·026

10 Which is the largest?

A ◯ 0·74   B ◯ 0·735   C ◯ 0·7168   D ◯ 0·70001   E ◯ 0·7399

11 The recurring decimal 0·166666... when expressed as a fraction is equivalent to:

A ◯ $\frac{1}{16}$ B ◯ $\frac{1}{3}$ C ◯ $\frac{1}{6}$ D ◯ $\frac{16}{100}$ E ◯ $\frac{1666}{10\,000}$

12 Which is the smallest?

A ◯ 0·5   B ◯ $(0·5)^2$ C ◯ 0·05   D ◯ $(0·5)^3$ E ◯ $(0·05)^2$

True or false?

Here are 60 number sentences. Check each one carefully to see whether it is true or false. Colour in the appropriate bubble for your answer.

		True	False				True	False
1	$(3 + 4) + 5 = 3 + (4 + 5)$	⬭	⬭	**2**	$(3 \times 4) + 5 = 3 \times (4 + 5)$	⬭	⬭
3	$(2 \times 3) \times 4 = 2 \times (3 \times 4)$	⬭	⬭	**4**	$(5 - 3) + 2 = 5 - (3 + 2)$	⬭	⬭
5	$(8 - 3) \times 2 = 8 - (3 \times 2)$	⬭	⬭	**6**	$(4 + 8) \times 2 = 4 + (8 \times 2)$	⬭	⬭
7	$3 \times 7 = 7 \times 3$	⬭	⬭	**8**	$4 \div 2 = 2 \div 4$	⬭	⬭
9	$(5 - 3) - 2 = 5 - (3 - 2)$	⬭	⬭	**10**	$(24 \div 6) - 4 = 24 \div (6 - 4)$	⬭	⬭
11	$(3 \times 10) \div 2 = 3 \times (10 \div 2)$	⬭	⬭	**12**	$6 \div 3 = 6 \times \frac{1}{3}$	⬭	⬭
13	$\frac{1}{2}$ of $14 = 14 \div 2$	⬭	⬭	**14**	$\frac{1}{2}$ of $20 = 20 \times \frac{1}{2}$	⬭	⬭
15	$\frac{1}{2}$ of $4 + \frac{1}{2}$ of $6 = \frac{1}{2}$ of $(4 + 6)$	⬭	⬭	**16**	$\frac{1}{2}$ of $12 + \frac{1}{2}$ of $4 = \frac{1}{2}$ of 16	⬭	⬭
17	$\frac{1}{4}$ of $12 + \frac{1}{4}$ of $12 = \frac{1}{2}$ of 12	⬭	⬭	**18**	$\frac{1}{4}$ of $16 + \frac{1}{4}$ of $16 = \frac{1}{2}$ of 16	⬭	⬭
19	$2^2 = 2 \times 2$	⬭	⬭	**20**	$3^2 + 4^2 = 5^2$	⬭	⬭
21	$2^2 + 3^2 = (2 + 3)^2$	⬭	⬭	**22**	$4^3 = 4 \times 4 \times 4$	⬭	⬭
23	$4^3 - 4^2 = 4$	⬭	⬭	**24**	$4^3 \div 4^2 = 4$	⬭	⬭
25	$9^2 - 2^2 = (9 - 2) \times (9 + 2)$	⬭	⬭	**26**	$10^2 - 5^2 = (10 - 5) \times (10 + 5)$	⬭	⬭
27	$9^2 - 3^2 = 6 \times 12$	⬭	⬭	**28**	$8^2 - 2^2 = 6 \times 10$	⬭	⬭
29	$7^2 - 3^2 = 4^2$	⬭	⬭	**30**	$100^2 - 1^2 = 101 \times 99$	⬭	⬭
31	$4 \times 9 - 4 \times 4 = 4 \times (9 - 4)$	⬭	⬭	**32**	$(12 - 5) \times 2 = 12 \times 2 - 5 \times 2$	⬭	⬭
33	$8 \times 3 - 5 \times 3 = (8 - 5) \times 3$	⬭	⬭	**34**	$3 \times 4 + 2 \times 4 = (3 + 2) \times 4$	⬭	⬭
35	$99 \times 7 + 99 \times 3 = 99 \times (7 + 3)$	⬭	⬭	**36**	$(30 \div 5) + (20 \div 5) = 50 \div 5$	⬭	⬭
37	$(30 \div 5) - (20 \div 5) = 10 \div 5$	⬭	⬭	**38**	$(12 \div 4) + (8 \div 4) = (12 + 8) \div 4$	⬭	⬭
39	$(20 \div 2) + (12 \div 2) = (20 + 12) \div 2$	⬭	⬭	**40**	$(3 + 4)^2 = 3^2 + 4^2 + 2 \times 3 \times 4$	⬭	⬭
41	$(5 + 2)^2 = 5^2 + 2^2$	⬭	⬭	**42**	$(5 + 2)^2 = 5^2 + 2^2 + 2 \times 5 \times 2$	⬭	⬭
43	$\frac{1}{3} < \frac{1}{4}$	⬭	⬭	**44**	$(\frac{1}{2})^2 < \frac{1}{4}$	⬭	⬭
45	$(\frac{1}{2})^2 < \frac{1}{2}$	⬭	⬭	**46**	$(\frac{2}{3})^2 > \frac{2}{3}$	⬭	⬭
47	$(\frac{3}{4})^2 < \frac{3}{4}$	⬭	⬭	**48**	$(\frac{2}{3})^2 < \frac{2}{3}$	⬭	⬭
49	$(\frac{1}{3} + \frac{1}{4})^2 < \frac{1}{2}$	⬭	⬭	**50**	$(3\frac{1}{2})^2 = 3 \times 4 + \frac{1}{4}$	⬭	⬭
51	$(4\frac{1}{2})^2 = 4 \times 5 + \frac{1}{4}$	⬭	⬭	**52**	$(5\frac{1}{2})^2 = 5 \times 6 + \frac{1}{4}$	⬭	⬭
53	$0 \cdot 4 < 4 \cdot 0$	⬭	⬭	**54**	$(0 \cdot 2)^2 = 0 \cdot 4$	⬭	⬭
55	$0 \cdot 4 \times 0 \cdot 3 = 1 \cdot 2$	⬭	⬭	**56**	$(0 \cdot 5)^2 = 0 \cdot 25$	⬭	⬭
57	$\triangle^2 = \triangle \times \triangle$	⬭	⬭	**58**	$(\triangle + \bigcirc) + \square = \triangle + (\bigcirc + \square)$	⬭	⬭
59	$\triangle^2 + \bigcirc^2 = (\triangle + \bigcirc)^2$	⬭	⬭	**60**	$\triangle - \bigcirc - \square = \triangle - (\bigcirc + \square)$	⬭	⬭

Number, Patterns & Algebra

8

Fraction fun

In these equations, some of the digits or fractions have been replaced by squares. Can you find the missing numbers?

1 $\frac{1}{2} \times \boxed{} = 10$

2 $\boxed{} \times 40 = 20$

3 $\frac{1}{3} \times \boxed{} = 4$

4 $\boxed{} \times 15 = 3$

5 $\frac{1}{10} \times \boxed{} = 5$

6 $\boxed{} \times 40 = 8$

7 $\boxed{} \times 24 = 4$

8 $\frac{1}{3} \times \boxed{} = 12$

9 $\frac{1}{5} \times \boxed{} = 5$

10 $\frac{1}{4} \times \boxed{} = 4$

11 $\frac{1}{4} \times \boxed{} = 6$

12 $\boxed{} \times 32 = 8$

13 $\boxed{} \times 27 = 9$

14 $\boxed{} \times 24 = 12$

15 $\boxed{} \times 24 = 8$

16 $\frac{2}{5} \times 20 = \boxed{}$

17 $\frac{3}{5} \times 45 = \boxed{}$

18 $\frac{3}{4} \times \boxed{} = 30$

19 $\frac{3}{4} \times \boxed{} = 12$

20 $\frac{3}{5} \times \boxed{} = 12$

21 $\frac{\boxed{}}{5} \times 20 = 8$

22 $\frac{\boxed{}}{10} \times 60 = 18$

23 $\frac{\boxed{}}{3} \times 12 = 8$

24 $\frac{\boxed{}}{4} \times 24 = 18$

25 $\frac{\boxed{}}{5} \times 25 = 15$

26 $\frac{3}{10} \times \boxed{} = 30$

27 $\frac{3}{10} \times \boxed{} = 12$

28 $\frac{3}{\boxed{}} \times 40 = 12$

29 $\frac{3}{\boxed{}} \times 40 = 30$

30 $\frac{3}{\boxed{}} \times 30 = 9$

Fraction challenges

1. In this exercise, each statement gives the clue to a number. (It could be a fraction.) Find the number in each case.

   a $\frac{1}{2}$ the number is 8. _____   **b** $\frac{1}{4}$ of the number is 8. _____

   c $\frac{3}{4}$ of the number is 12. _____   **d** $\frac{2}{3}$ of the number is 18. _____

   e $\frac{2}{7}$ of the number is 14. _____   **f** $\frac{9}{10}$ of the number is 90. _____

   g $\frac{3}{5}$ of the number is 30. _____   **h** $\frac{4}{3}$ of the number is 24. _____

   i $\frac{1}{2}$ the number plus 5 is the same as the number itself. _____

   j $\frac{1}{2}$ the number plus 8 is the same as the number itself. _____

   k If you halve the number and subtract 4, the answer is 2. _____

   l If you double the number and subtract $\frac{1}{2}$, the answer is 2. _____

   m If you double the number and add $\frac{1}{2}$, the answer is 2. _____

   n If you add the number to double its own value, the answer is 1. _____

   o If you multiply the number by 4 and add 5, the answer is 7. _____

2. Find two numbers whose sum is 1 and whose difference is $\frac{1}{2}$. _____

3. Find two numbers whose sum is 1 and whose difference is $\frac{1}{3}$. _____

4. Find two numbers whose sum is 2 and whose difference is 1. _____

5. Find a fraction whose square is greater than itself. $\square^2 > \square$ _____
   How many solutions can you find? _____

6. Find a fraction whose square is smaller than itself. $\square^2 < \square$ _____
   How many solutions can you find? _____

Egyptian fractions

The Egyptians wrote all their fractions so that they had a numerator of 1.
For example examine these fractions and their Egyptian equivalents.

$$\frac{3}{4} = \frac{1}{2} + \frac{1}{4} \qquad \frac{2}{3} = \frac{1}{2} + \frac{1}{6}$$

Note the easiest way to do this is to use equivalent fractions so that:

$$\frac{2}{3} = \frac{4}{6} = \frac{3}{6} + \frac{1}{6} = \frac{1}{2} + \frac{1}{6}$$

7. Write the following fractions as their Egyptian equivalents.

   a $\frac{5}{8}$ _____   **b** $\frac{6}{10}$ _____

   c $\frac{5}{6}$ _____   **d** $\frac{7}{10}$ _____

   e $\frac{7}{12}$ _____   **f** $\frac{11}{15}$ _____

Find the fraction

1 In the following equations, some numbers have been replaced with different shapes. Find the value of each shape.

a $\dfrac{2}{\square} = \dfrac{\square}{8}$ _____

b $\dfrac{2}{\bigstar} = \dfrac{\bigstar}{18}$ _____

c $\dfrac{3}{\bigcirc} = \dfrac{\bigcirc}{12}$ _____

d $\dfrac{3}{\diamondsuit} = \dfrac{\diamondsuit}{27}$ _____

e $\dfrac{4}{\#} = \dfrac{\#}{36}$ _____

f $\dfrac{2}{\bigcirc} = \dfrac{\bigcirc}{32}$ _____

g $3 \times \dfrac{1}{\square} = 1$ _____

h $\pentagon \times \dfrac{1}{5} = 1$ _____

i $\dfrac{\odot}{\square} \times \dfrac{2}{5} = 1$ _____

j $\dfrac{4}{\bigcirc} \times \dfrac{\square}{7} = 1$ _____

2 **a** Find the average of $\frac{1}{2}$ and $\frac{1}{3}$. _____

b Find the average of $\frac{1}{2}$, $\frac{1}{3}$ and $\frac{1}{6}$. _____

3 Find the square root of:

a $2\frac{1}{4}$ _____

b $5\frac{1}{16}$ _____

c $1\frac{7}{9}$ _____

4 Express each of the following as a simple fraction in lowest terms.

a $1 \div \left(1 \div \frac{1}{3}\right)$ _____

b $1 \div \left(1 \div \frac{1}{5}\right)$ _____

c $1 \div \left(1 \div \frac{3}{5}\right)$ _____

d $\dfrac{1}{1 + \frac{1}{2}}$ _____

e $\dfrac{1}{1 + \frac{1}{1 + \frac{1}{2}}}$ _____

f $\dfrac{1}{2 + \frac{1}{2}}$ _____

g $\dfrac{1}{2 + \frac{1}{2 + \frac{1}{2}}}$ _____

h $\dfrac{1}{1 + \frac{1}{1 - \frac{1}{4}}}$ _____

5 Simplify each fraction. Draw a box around the greatest and a circle around the least fraction in each group.

a $\dfrac{3}{4}$ $\dfrac{3+1}{4+1}$ _____ $\dfrac{3+2}{4+2}$ _____ $\dfrac{3+3}{4+3}$ _____ $\dfrac{3-2}{4-2}$ _____

b $\dfrac{5}{2}$ $\dfrac{5+1}{2+1}$ _____ $\dfrac{5+2}{2+2}$ _____ $\dfrac{5+3}{2+3}$ _____ $\dfrac{5-1}{2-1}$ _____

c $\dfrac{3}{8}$ $\dfrac{3+1}{8+1}$ _____ $\dfrac{3+2}{8+2}$ _____ $\dfrac{3+12}{8+12}$ _____ $\dfrac{3-2}{8-2}$ _____

Spending money

1 Jordon had a sum of money. In each question below (with the use of a diagram) work out how much he started with if:

a After he spent $\frac{1}{2}$ of the original sum on a present, and he put $\frac{1}{2}$ of the remainder in the bank he had $12 left. _____

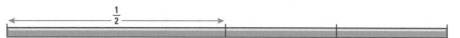

b After he spent $\frac{1}{3}$ of his money on a present, and he put $\frac{1}{2}$ of the remainder in the bank he had $24 left. _____

c After he spent $\frac{1}{2}$ on a present, and he put $\frac{1}{3}$ of the remainder in the bank, he had $12 left. _____

d After he spent $\frac{1}{2}$ on a present, he put $\frac{1}{3}$ of the remainder in the bank and then he spent $\frac{1}{2}$ of what is left at the movies. He now had $8 left. _____

e After he spent $\frac{1}{3}$ of his money on a present, and he spent $\frac{1}{4}$ of the remainder on a book, he has $36 remaining. _____

2 Gina spent $\frac{1}{3}$ of her money on a present. Next she spent $\frac{1}{4}$ of the remainder on a book. If she spent $\frac{1}{3}$ of what is left at the movies she still had $16 left.

a How much did Gina spend at the movies? _____

b How much did Gina have at the start? _____

3 Justin spent $\frac{1}{4}$ of his money on a present. Next he spent $\frac{1}{6}$ of the remainder on a book. He has $50 remaining.

a How much was the book? _____

b How much money did Justin have at the start? _____

Number, Patterns & Algebra

Consecutive numbers

Consecutive numbers are numbers that follow in order, such as 7, 8, 9 or 11, 12, 13.

Consecutive *even* numbers are even numbers that follow in order, such as 2, 4, 6 or 22, 24, 26.

Consecutive *odd* numbers are odd numbers that follow in order, such as 1, 3, 5, or 11, 13, 15.

1   What *consecutive* numbers are described in each case below?

    a   Two numbers whose sum is 23   _____ _____

    b   Three numbers whose sum is 27   _____ _____ _____

    c   Two numbers whose product is 42   _____ _____

    d   Three numbers whose product is 60   _____ _____ _____

    e   Three even numbers whose sum is 54   _____ _____ _____

    f   Two odd numbers whose sum is 40   _____ _____

    g   Three numbers whose sum is 75   _____ _____ _____

    h   Three odd numbers whose sum is 75.   _____ _____ _____

2   Try a lot of examples before answering these questions, and explain your reasoning.

    a   Is the sum of two consecutive numbers always divisible by 2? _____

    b   Is the product of two consecutive numbers always divisible by 2? _____

    c   Is the product of three consecutive numbers always divisible by 3? _____

    d   Is the product of three consecutive numbers always divisible by 6? _____

3   Consider three consecutive numbers. Work out the square of the middle number minus the product of the other two numbers.

    For example: 4, 5, 6 $5 \times 5 - 4 \times 6$ = 25 − 24
                                                      = 1

                  9, 10, 11 $10 \times 10 - 9 \times 11$ = 100 − 99
                                                         = 1

    Try this with other numbers. What result do you find? _____

4   Consider:

    a   three consecutive even numbers;

    b   three consecutive odd numbers.

    Investigate what happens in each case if you work out the square of the middle number minus the product of the other two numbers.

Factorial notation

The expression 7!, factorial 7, is mathematical shorthand for $7 \times 6 \times 5 \times 4 \times 3 \times 2 \times 1$ and it equals the products of all the whole numbers less than and equal to itself.

Similarly, 4! is mathematical shorthand for $4 \times 3 \times 2 \times 1$.

To simplify: $= \dfrac{4!}{3!} = \dfrac{4 \times 3 \times 2 \times 1}{3 \times 2 \times 1}$

$= 4$

1 Simplify these expressions.

a $\dfrac{5!}{4!}$ _____

b $\dfrac{6!}{5!}$ _____

c $\dfrac{7!}{6!}$ _____

d $\dfrac{10!}{9!}$ _____

e $\dfrac{20!}{9!}$ _____

f $\dfrac{5!}{3!}$ _____

g $\dfrac{6!}{4!}$ _____

h $\dfrac{10!}{8!}$ _____

To simplify $9! \div 9$ and express the answer in factorial notation:

$\dfrac{9!}{9} = \dfrac{9 \times 8 \times 7 \times 6 \times 5 \times 4 \times 3 \times 2 \times 1}{9}$

$= 8 \times 7 \times 6 \times 5 \times 4 \times 3 \times 2 \times 1$

$= 8!$

2 Simplify these expressions, giving each answer in factorial notation.

a $5! \div 5$ _____

b $8! \div 8$ _____

c $10! \div 10$ _____

d $\dfrac{10!}{10 \times 9}$ _____

e $\dfrac{10!}{10 \times 9 \times 8}$ _____

f $\dfrac{12!}{12 \times 11}$ _____

g $\dfrac{12!}{12 \times 11 \times 10}$ _____

h $\dfrac{20!}{20 \times 19}$ _____

i $\dfrac{20!}{20 \times 19 \times 18}$ _____

j $\dfrac{20!}{20 \times 19 \times 18 \times 17}$ _____

3 Show that each line in the following pattern is true. Continue the pattern for the next two lines.

$1 \times 1! = 2! - 1$

$1 \times 1! + 2 \times 2! = 3! - 1$

$1 \times 1! + 2 \times 2! + 3 \times 3! = 4! - 1$

_____

_____

Four 4s problem

Using the digit 4 exactly four times in each sentence together with the mathematical symbols +, −, ×, ÷, ( ) or $\sqrt{\ }$, write mathematically true sentences for as many of the numbers from 0 to 100 as you can. (If you can find sentences for 85 numbers, it will be an excellent effort.)

Do not forget the order of operations:

Work brackets first.

Multiply and divide before you add and subtract:

$$4 \times 4 + 4 \div 4 = 16 + 1$$
$$= 17$$

The following will be very useful.

$\sqrt{4}$ means 'the square root of 4'. $\sqrt{4} = 2$

You may use 44; for example, $15 = 44 \div 4 + 4$

$4! = 4 \times 3 \times 2 \times 1$
  $= 24$

4^4 means $4 \times 4 \times 4 \times 4$, and since $\sqrt{4} = 2$,
then $(\sqrt{4})^4 = \sqrt{4} \times \sqrt{4} \times \sqrt{4} \times \sqrt{4} = 16$

$\dfrac{4}{\cdot 4} = 4 \div \dfrac{4}{10} = 10$

$44 \div \cdot 4 = 110$

$4 \cdot 4 \div \cdot 4 = 11$

$\sqrt{4} \div \cdot 4 = 2 \div \dfrac{4}{10} = 5$

$\cdot \dot{4}$ means $\cdot 44444 \ldots$, and its mathematical value is $\dfrac{4}{9}$.

So $\dfrac{4}{\cdot \dot{4}} = 4 \div \dfrac{4}{9} = 9$

$4! \div \cdot 4 = 24 \times \dfrac{10}{4} = 60$

$4! \div \cdot \dot{4} = 24 \times \dfrac{9}{4} = 54$

$(4! + 4) \div \cdot 4 = 28 \times \dfrac{10}{4} = 70$

$(4! + \sqrt{4}) \div \cdot 4 = 26 \times \dfrac{10}{4} = 65$

$(4! + 4) \div \cdot \dot{4} = 28 \times \dfrac{9}{4} = 63$

Therefore $4! - 4 + \sqrt{4} \times \sqrt{4} = 24 - 4 + 4 = 24$

$4 \div \cdot 4 + 4! \div \sqrt{4} = 10 + 12 = 32$

$(4 \div \cdot 4 + 4!) \div \sqrt{4} = 34 \div 2 = 17$

Sequences

1 In the sequence 2, 5, 8, ..., 2 is the 1st term, 5 is the 2nd, and 8 is the 3rd. To find the 9th term, we add 8 times 3 to 2, as each term is 3 more than the previous term.

a Find the 12th and 25th terms of this sequence without listing all the terms. _____ and _____

Use the same method to find the terms listed in questions **b** to **j**.

	Terms	aSequence	Numbers
b	12th and 30th	3, 8, 13, 18 ...	_____ and _____
c	15th and 50th	1, 7, 13, 19 ...	_____ and _____
d	8th and 25th	16, 23, 30, 37 ...	_____ and _____
e	11th and 31st	2, 11, 20, 29 ...	_____ and _____
f	9th and 40th	11, 15, 19, 23 ...	_____ and _____
g	11th and 21st	197, 192, 187, 182 ...	_____ and _____
h	13th and 26th	183, 179, 175, 171 ...	_____ and _____
i	5th and 8th	1, 2, 4, 8 ...	_____ and _____
j	6th and 8th	$\frac{1}{9}, \frac{1}{3}, 1, 3$ ...	_____ and _____

2 Find the first five terms of the sequence in which:

a The first number is 2 and the fourth is 8. _____

b The first number is 1 and the fourth is 10. _____

c The second number is 5 and the fifth is 11. _____

d The first number is 2 and the fifth is 22. _____

e The second number is 6 and the fifth is 18. _____

f The second number is 10 and the fourth is 24. _____

g The third number is 14 and the fifth is 26. _____

h The second number is 9 and the fourth is 25. _____

i The first number is 51 and the third is 43. _____

j The second number is 43 and the fifth is 28. _____

Bartering

Sometimes people swap or exchange goods without using money.
This system of trading is called 'barter'.

At one barter market, the following values have been established:
12 carrots = 6 bananas = 3 oranges = 4 apples = 1 pineapple
so that 2 pineapples are worth 8 apples or 6 oranges or 12 bananas or 24 carrots.

1 How many pineapples will I need in each case if I want to obtain:

   a 12 bananas _____   **b** 36 carrots _____

   c 12 apples _____   **d** 15 oranges _____

   e 36 oranges? _____

2 If I have 120 carrots, how many of each of these other fruits can I obtain?

   a oranges _____   **b** apples _____

   c bananas _____

3 How many apples will I need in each case if I want to obtain:

   a 5 pineapples _____   **b** 15 oranges _____

   c 12 bananas _____   **d** 3 bananas _____

   e 36 carrots? _____

4 I want to obtain 60 carrots. Suggest three different examples of what I could give in exchange.

   _____ or _____ or _____

5 If I have 12 oranges and 12 apples, how many bananas can I obtain? _____

6 If I have 9 oranges, 24 bananas and 8 apples,
how many pineapples can I trade them for? _____

7 If I have 18 carrots and 3 bananas, how many pineapples can I obtain? _____

Percentage challenges

1 Increase 60 by 50%. _____

2 Find the number that when increased by 50% becomes 24. _____

3 Decrease 60 by 50%. _____

4 Find the number that when decreased by 50% becomes 18. _____

5 Find the number that when decreased by 25% becomes 18. _____

6 Increase 50 by 20%. _____

7 Find the number that when increased by 20% becomes 30. _____

8 Decrease 50 by 20%. _____

9 Find the number that when decreased by 20% becomes 32. _____

10 Increase 24 by $33\frac{1}{3}$%. _____

11 Find the number that when increased by $33\frac{1}{3}$% becomes 48. _____

12 Find the number that when decreased by $33\frac{1}{3}$% becomes 48. _____

13 20% of a certain number is 12. What is the number? _____

14 5% of a certain number is 3. What is the number? _____

15 15% of a certain number is 21. What is the number? _____

16 2% of a certain number is 5. What is the number? _____

17 30% of a certain number is 12. What is the number? _____

18 60% of a certain number is 12. What is the number? _____

19 Yvonne was given 80% for her spelling test. She had spelled 48 words correctly and all the words were of equal value. How many words were there in the test?

_____

20 A dealer sold a car for $12 000 and made a profit of 25%. (Note that here selling price = cost price + profit.) How much did the car cost the dealer? _____

21 By selling his car for $12 000, Mr Green lost 25%. (Note that here selling price = cost price − loss.) How much did Mr Green pay for his car? _____

22 An insurance company paid $320 to Heather in compensation for her stolen camera. If this was 80% of its value, what was Heather's camera worth? _____

Number, Patterns & Algebra

Percentage problems

1 Every employee at a certain store is entitled to a discount of 10% on selling prices. At a sale, every item was reduced by 10%.

Is an employee entitled to a 20% discount on a dress that originally cost $150? Explain your answer.

_____   _____
_____   _____
_____   _____

2 In a certain country you must pay a 15% sales tax on every item you purchase.

In a sale, a 20% discount is offered on all items.

Which would you prefer to have calculated first—discount or tax?

(**Hint**: Work on an item with a base cost of $100.)

_____   _____
_____   _____
_____   _____

3 A car dealer bought two used cars but found himself short of money and had to resell them quickly. He sold them both for $18 000 each. On one car he made a profit of 20% and on the other he lost 20%.

Did he make or lose money on the whole deal? In either case, how much?

_____   _____
_____   _____
_____   _____

4 Joseph pays $1000 for a painting for his art gallery. He sells it to a customer at a 25% profit. Some time later this customer sells the painting back to Joseph at a 25% loss, and Joseph then sells it to another customer for $1100.

How much profit did Joseph make on this painting altogether?

_____   _____
_____   _____
_____   _____

5 Glenn sells an article to Beverly at a profit of 20%. Beverly sells the same article to Edgar at a profit of 50%.

If Edgar pays $270 for the article, for what price did Glenn buy it?

_____   _____
_____   _____
_____   _____

Fruit arithmetic

In these operations fruits have replaced many of the numbers. Note that the value of specific fruits varies between exercises.

Find all the different values.

1

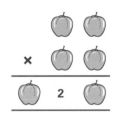

2

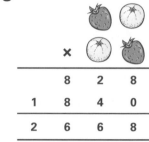

		1	0	5
	1	7	5	0
	1	8	5	5

3

		8	2	8
	1	8	4	0
	2	6	6	8

4

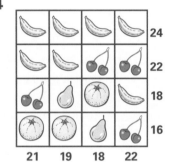

5

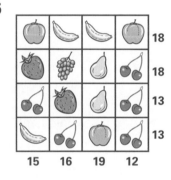

6

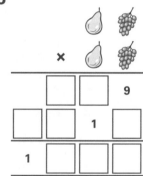

7

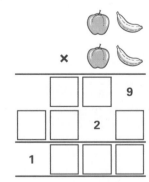

8

9

10

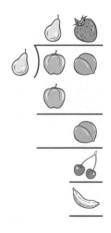

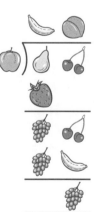

Divisibility number puzzles

1   I am thinking of a number. It is both a triangular number and a square number. It is less than 60.

What is the number?   _____

2   Write down the smallest number that is exactly divisible by every number from:

a   2 to 5   _____   **b**   2 to 6   _____

c   2 to 7   _____   **d**   2 to 8   _____

3   What is the smallest number that leaves a remainder of 1 when:

a   it is divided by 2, and a remainder of 2 when it is divided by 3?   _____

b   it is divided by 2, 3 or 4?   _____

c   it is divided by 2, 3, 4 or 5?   _____

d   it is divided by 2, 3, 4, 5 or 6?   _____

4   What is the smallest number that leaves a remainder of 1 when it is divided by 2, 3, 4, 5, 6 or 8?   _____

5   A group of children at a party found they were able to play games that required them to play in pairs or in groups of 3, 4 or 8. However, when they wanted to play a game that needed a group of 5, then 4 children were left out.

How many children were at the party?   _____

6   A farmer has a number of rabbits and rabbit hutches. If 5 rabbits are placed in each hutch, 2 rabbits are left over. If 6 rabbits are placed in each hutch, one hutch is left empty.

How many rabbits and how many hutches does the farmer have?

_____ rabbits,   _____ hutches

7   Find the value of the digits A and B in each of the following.

a   A54B is divisible by 12   _____ _____

b   A9543B is divisible by 11 and 8   _____ _____

8   Find the smallest number that is divisible by each of the numbers 6, 8, 9 and 12.   _____

Money problems

1 Felicity bought a TV set for $850. She paid a deposit of $130, and the remaining amount was paid in 12 equal monthly instalments.
How much did Felicity pay each month? _____

2 Ingrid bought a stereo system for $600. She first paid a deposit and then paid a $40 instalment each month. If the stereo was paid for in 12 months, how much deposit did Ingrid pay? _____

3 Many years ago, telegrams were used to send urgent messages. The cost of a telegram depended on the number of words sent; the charge was $2.40 for the first 6 words and 30c for each additional word.

   a What was the price of a telegram that had 21 words? _____

   b If it cost $5.70 to send a telegram, how many words were in the message? _____

4 To send large parcels overseas, a firm charges $32 for the first 10 kg and $8 for each additional 5 kg or part thereof. This means that if a parcel has a mass of 17 kg, the charge would be:

     $32 for 10 kg
     $8 for the next 5 kg
     $8 for the next 2 kg (as it is part of 5 kg)
     ∴ $48 for 17 kg

   a How much would it cost to send a 28 kg parcel? _____

   b If the firm charged a person $80, what was the mass of the parcel? _____

5 Mrs King earned $1250. She gave $\frac{1}{5}$ of this amount to her husband and $\frac{1}{4}$ of the remainder she put in the bank.
How much does she have left? _____

6 Georgina and Evelyn had a total of $56. If one-third of Georgina's money is equal to one quarter of Evelyn's, how much more money than Georgina does Evelyn have? Use this diagram to help you. _____

    Georgina
    Evelyn

Number, Patterns & Algebra

Use your calculator

1 Sylvia earns $500 each week.
How much does she earn in a year? _____

2 Graham earns $31 200 in a year.
How much does he earn each week? _____

3 Lynda earns $16 an hour in her job. If she works 8 hours each day for 5 days a week, how much will she earn:

a in a day? _____   **b** in a week? _____

4 Helen wanted to buy a mobile phone for $200. She only had $50 for a deposit. For the rest of the money she owed she had to pay $15 every week for 12 weeks.

a How much did the phone cost her? _____

b The extra she paid is called interest.
How much interest did she pay? _____

5 Penny bought a DVD recorder for $850. She did not have to pay a deposit and she made 36 payments of $30 each month.

a What was the total of the monthly payments? _____

b How much interest did Penny pay? _____

6 Garry works 40 hours a week at $18.50 an hour. Nicky works 35 hours at $21.20 an hour.

a How much does Garry earn in a week? _____

b How much does Nicky earn in a week? _____

c Who has the greater weekly wage? _____

d What is the difference in their weekly earnings? _____

7 A shop sells a plasma television for $5000 cash or it can be bought on terms. Brian bought the television on terms of $800 deposit and $160 per month for 3 years.

a What was the total amount Brian paid for the television? _____

b How much interest did he pay? _____

Tessa's world trip

1 Tessa's first stop is England, where the exchange rate is 40p for A$1, or £1 for A$2.50.

   a She exchanges A$800 at the airport when she arrives. How many pounds is she given? _____

   b Her hotel room costs her £80 a night. How much is that in Australian dollars? _____

   c She decides to go on a coach tour of Wales, which costs her £112. How much is that in Australian dollars? _____

2 Tessa now flies to France, where the exchange rate is 3 Euros for A$5.

   a She exchanges A$400. How many Euros does she get? _____

   b She buys lunch for 36 Euros. How much would this be in Australian dollars? _____

   c She goes on two sightseeing tours costing 120 Euros. How much would this have cost in Australian dollars? _____

3 Sweden is the next country that Tessa visits. Here the exchange rate is 6 kronor for A$1.

   a She exchanges A$300. How many kronor is this? _____

   b She buys a handbag for 240 kronor. How much would this be in Australian dollars? _____

   c Her accommodation costs her 1500 kronor. How many Australian dollars is this? _____

4 In Hungary the exchange rate is 150 forints for $A1.

   a If she exchanges A$200, how many forints does she get? _____

   b She pays 9900 forints for a coach tour. How much is that in Australian dollars? _____

5 In India the exchange rate is 30 rupees for A$1.

   a She exchanges A$200. How many rupees does she get? _____

   b She buys lunch, which costs her 375 rupees. How many Australian dollars is this? _____

6 Tessa flies to the United States of America before returning to Australia. The exchange rate is US$0.75 for A$1.

   a What is US$1 worth in Australian dollars? _____

   b She exchanges A$800. How many US dollars does she get? _____

   c She buys a pair of shoes for US$60. How much is this in Australian dollars? _____

   d How many US dollars would Tessa get if she exchanged A$480 later in her trip? _____

   e If Tessa signed up for a bus tour for US$300, how much is this costing her in Australian dollars? _____

Number, Patterns & Algebra

Hiring a bus

1 The Friendly bus company charges $250 for the hire of a bus for a morning and $2 for each student.

    a How much would the school pay to the bus company for a group of 25 students? _____

    b How much should the school charge each of these 25 students to recover their cost? _____

    c How much would the school pay to the bus company for a group of 15 students? _____

    d How much would the school pay to the bus company for a group of 45 students? _____

2 The Economy bus company charges $150 for the hire of a bus for a morning and $5 for each student.

    a How much would the school pay to the bus company for a group of 25 students? _____

    b How much should the school charge each of these 25 students to recover their cost? _____

    c How much would the school pay to the bus company for a group of 15 students? _____

    d How much would the school pay to the bus company for a group of 45 students? _____

3 Travelsafe bus company charges $11 for each student for a minimum of 20 students.

    a How much would the school pay to the bus company for a group of 25 students? _____

    b How much would the school pay to the bus company for a group of 45 students? _____

4 Consider the above bus companies' charges for bus hire.

    a If 25 students were going on an excursion, which bus company is cheaper?

    _____

    b If 45 students were going on an excursion, which bus company is cheaper?

    _____

    c If 35 students were going on an excursion, which bus company is cheaper?

    _____

Matchstick puzzles

Carefully draw the next shape to continue the sequence.

Complete the table and look for a pattern from which you can predict the number of matches needed for the tenth diagram. In your own words, describe the pattern in each exercise.

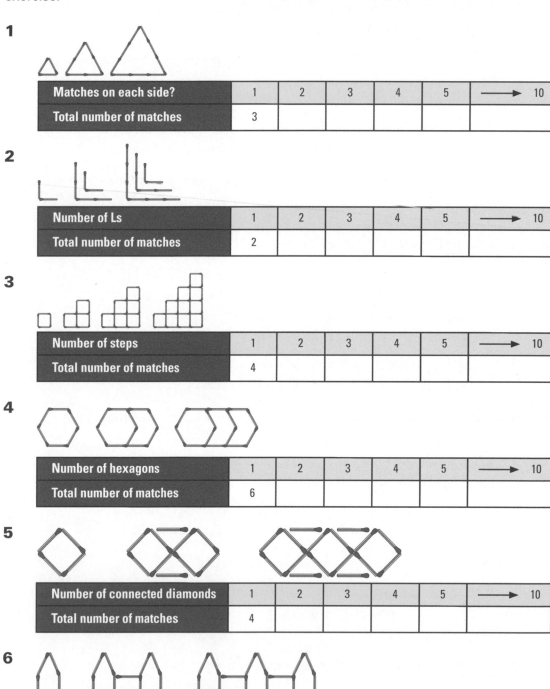

1

Matches on each side?	1	2	3	4	5	→ 10
Total number of matches	3					

2

Number of Ls	1	2	3	4	5	→ 10
Total number of matches	2					

3

Number of steps	1	2	3	4	5	→ 10
Total number of matches	4					

4

Number of hexagons	1	2	3	4	5	→ 10
Total number of matches	6					

5

Number of connected diamonds	1	2	3	4	5	→ 10
Total number of matches	4					

6

Number of pentagon patterns	1	2	3	4	5	→ 10
Total number of matches	5					

Number, Patterns & Algebra

Patterns with squares

There are several ways of enlarging squares, making various patterns.

Draw the next figure in each pattern. Write below it the number of extra squares you needed. Then write down the two numbers following in the sequence.

1

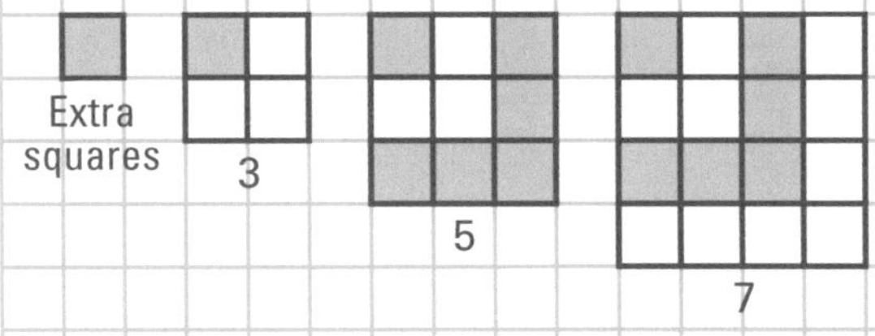

Extra squares   3   5   7

2

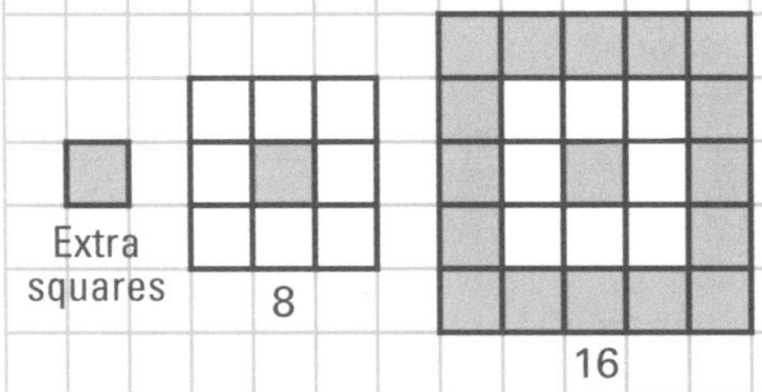

Extra squares   8   16

3

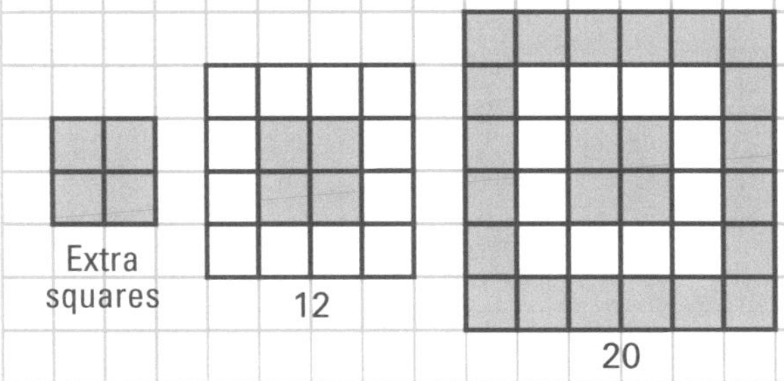

Extra squares   12   20

4

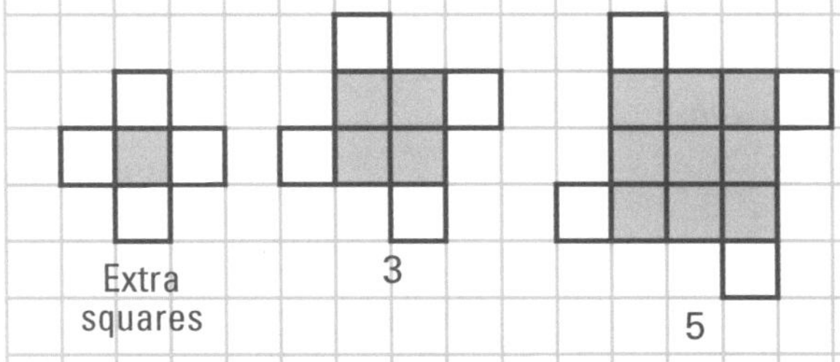

Extra squares   3   5

Counting techniques

It may be helpful to use tree diagrams in solving these problems.

1 Work out how many 2-digit numbers can be formed from the digits 3, 4 and 5:

  a if repetition of the digits is not allowed; _____

  b if repetition is allowed. _____

2 Mrs Kelly has four cards. Each card has one of the numbers 3, 5, 7 or 8 on it.

| 3 | 5 | 7 | 8 |

  a How many different 2-digit numbers can she make? _____

  b How many different even 2-digit numbers can she make? _____

  c How many different 3-digit numbers can she make? _____

  d How many different even 3-digit numbers can she make? _____

  e How many different odd 3-digit numbers can she make? _____

  f How many different 4-digit numbers can she make? _____

  g How many different even 4-digit numbers can she make? _____

  h How many different odd 4-digit numbers can she make? _____

  i How many different 3-digit numbers
  which are divisible by 5 can she make? _____

  j How many different 2-digit numbers
  which are divisible by 3 can she make? _____

  k How many different 3-digit numbers
  which are divisible by 3 can she make? _____

3 Two young couples (Aa, Bb) go to the movies and sit in a row. If neither couple wishes to be separated, how many possible seating arrangements are there?

_____

4 Three young couples (Aa, Bb, Cc) go to the movies and sit in a row. How many possible seating arrangements are there if:

  a neither couple wishes to be separated and
  couple Aa insists on sitting near the aisle? _____

  b the three women and the three men wish to sit
  together and the women insist on sitting near the aisle? _____

Chance & Data

Number plates

1   In a small village, A, car number plates use the digits 0, 1, 2, ..., 9, and all have two digits—for example, 33, 44, 09. By the time all possible number plates have been used, how many cars will there be in this village?

                     _____

2   If in a neighbouring village, B, number plates have three digits and all possible three-digit combinations have been used, how many cars are there in village B?

                     _____

3   In village C, number plates have one letter (A–Z) followed by two digits. Work out how many number plates will:

    a   end in 00; _____

    b   end in 78; _____

    c   start with the letter B; _____

    d   start with the letter X; _____

    e   start with P8; _____

    f   be possible altogether. _____

4   In village D, number plates have two letters followed by two digits. Find out how many number plates will:

    a   end in A00; _____   **b**   end in 99; _____

    c   start with XX; _____   **d**   be possible altogether. _____

5   Number plates in most large cities have three letters followed by three numbers. Work out how many of these would:

    a   end in A000; _____   **b**   end in 123; _____

    c   begin with DAD; _____   **d**   be possible altogether. _____

Listing possibilities

1 In how many ways can you change a $1 coin into 50c, 20c and 10c coins? Illustrate this in a table.

2 Debbie asks a shopkeeper to change 50c into 20c, 10c and 5c coins only.

Draw up a table to list all possible ways in which she could be given change.

3 Mr Helpful is making the children's sandwiches in the morning. He plans to use white bread or brown bread and the fillings he has available are egg, cheese, tuna and honey. List the various sandwiches he can make if he puts only one type of filling in each sandwich.

4 A group of girls enter a tennis tournament. Each player plays every other competitor once.

Work out how many games must be played if the tournament is entered by:

a 3 girls _____   **b** 4 girls _____

c 5 girls _____   **d** 6 girls. _____

List the players as A, B, C and so on or draw a diagram.

Now look for a pattern in your findings.

e Can you predict how many games must be played in a tournament entered by 10 girls? _____

5 **a** Three friends—Jill, Marcia and Amanda—always send good-luck cards to each other before their exams.

How many cards will be exchanged altogether? _____

b If a fourth friend, Betty, joins in, how many cards will be sent altogether? _____

c If a fifth friend, Niki, joins the group, how many cards will be sent altogether? _____

d Try to predict how many good-luck cards there will be if 20 friends all sent them to each other. _____

6 Anatoly is playing a board game in which he has to roll two dice.

a What is the smallest sum that he can roll? _____

b With how many combinations can he roll:

i a sum of 8? _____   **ii** a sum of 9? _____

iii a sum of 10? _____   **iv** a sum of 11? _____

v a sum of 12? _____

Possibilities

Remember to work systematically.

1 In your purse you have $1.00 made up of seven coins. What coins are they?

_____

2 Paul has a $2 coin and needs one 20c coin for a parking meter. He asks a shop assistant for change, explaining that he must have at least one 20c coin and the rest can be any combination of $1, 50c and 10c coins. How many different value combinations can the shop assistant give Paul? (There are more than 20 possibilities.) Draw up a table to work this out.

3 **a** If each half of a domino is either blank or has 1, 2, 3, 4, 5 or 6 dots on it, and a set of dominoes ranges from double blank to double six, how many are there in a set? _____

b How many dominoes have 4 dots on one half? _____

c How many dots are there in a complete set of dominoes? _____

4 If I number the pages of a 36-page book, how many digits do I write? _____

5 How many pages does a book have if in numbering them I use:

a 129 digits? _____   **b** 204 digits? _____

6 A palindromic number is one that reads the same both forwards and backwards—for instance, 797 or 44.
How many palindromic numbers are there between:

a 10 and 400? _____   **b** 10 and 1000? _____

7 **a** How many numbers between 10 and 99 have two different digits? _____

b How many even numbers between 10 and 99 have two different digits? _____

c How many odd numbers between 10 and 99 have two different digits? _____

d How many numbers between 100 and 200 have three different digits? _____

8 In how many different ways can two different numbers be selected from the set {3, 4, 5, 6, 7} such that the sum of the numbers is:

a an even number? _____   **b** an odd number? _____

What's the chance?

1 An octahedron has the numbers from 1 to 8 written on its 8 faces. When an octahedron is rolled, a number on a face on top can be read as shown in the diagram.

If you roll two octahedrons and find the sum of the two numbers on the top faces, you will get the numbers in the table below. First complete the table below and then answer the following questions.

a What is the total number of possibilities? _____

b What is the least likely total? _____

c What is the most likely total? _____

d What is the chance of having a total of:

    i 2 _____   **ii** 4 _____   **iii** 9? _____

e Which two totals are equally likely? _____ _____

+	1	2	3	4	5	6	7	8
1	2	3	4	5				
2	3	4	5	6				
3	4	5	6	7				
4								
5								
6								
7								
8								

2 A dart is thrown at each of the dartboards shown. Write down the chance of the dart landing in each lettered section indicated in the diagram.

    a A   **b** B   **c** C   **d** A or B

i	ii	iii	iv	v

A _____   A _____   A _____   A _____   A _____

B _____   B _____   B _____   B _____   B _____

C _____   C _____   C _____   C _____   C _____

D _____   D _____   D _____   D _____   D _____

Chance and data

1 **a** Julian turns on the tap for 10 minutes, filling the bathtub to a height of 30 cm. He then sits in the bath, raising the water level by another 10 cm. He relaxes and plays in the bath for 10 minutes before getting out and pulling out the plug. It takes 5 minutes for the water to be emptied from the bath. Draw this information on graph i. (Looking at graph ii might help you.)

   b Make up a story that could explain the information shown in graph ii.

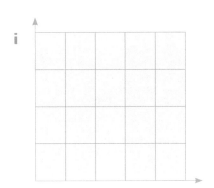

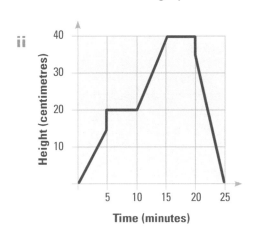

2 The results of a survey of shoe sizes for 12-year-old students are given below.

Shoe size	5	$5\frac{1}{2}$	6	$6\frac{1}{2}$	7	$7\frac{1}{2}$	8	$8\frac{1}{2}$
Number	2	5	12	15	11	8	4	3

   a Complete the column graph below to show this information.

   b What is the total number of children who were surveyed? _____

   c What fraction of students wear a size 6 shoe? _____

   d What percentage of students wear a size 6? _____

   e If a student is picked at random, what is the chance that he or she wears a size $7\frac{1}{2}$ or bigger shoe? _____

   f What percentage of 12-year-old students wear a size $7\frac{1}{2}$ shoe or larger? _____

   g If Amy gets a pair of shoes as a present and they are size $5\frac{1}{2}$, what is the chance that they will fit her? _____

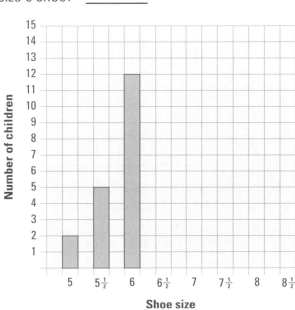

Interpreting graphs

1 Read the graph to answer these questions.

    a Who was the winner of this race? _____

    b Who came last in the race? _____

2 Who is represented by each point on the graph accompanying this illustration?

Write the first letter of the name under each number.

3 Who is represented by each point on the following graphs?

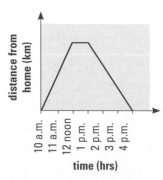

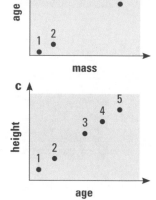

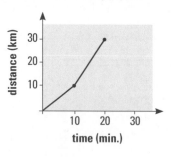

4 Describe the information contained in these graphs.

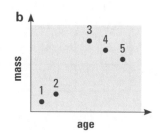

5 In England, the cost of a phone call depends (even for local calls) on the time taken as well as the distance covered.

A brief long-distance conversation could cost the same as a lengthy local call.

Explain what information this graph gives you.

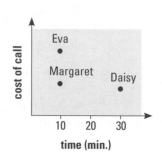

Graphs

1 Draw a graph showing a cyclist travelling from home at a constant speed of 30 km/hr for 2 hours, then resting for 1 hour.

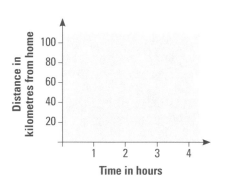

2 The height and age of Jesse and Greg have been graphed. Ivan is younger than Jesse and taller than Greg.

a Which point on the graph could represent Ivan? _____

b Compare the age and height of C and D, and then A and C.

_____

_____

_____

3 Water flows from two hoses into two tanks.

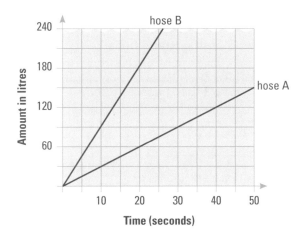

a How many litres of water flow from hose A in 50 seconds? _____

b How many seconds does it take hose B to fill tank B with 90 litres of water? _____

c How much more water flows from hose B than from hose A in 20 seconds? _____

d By studying the graph carefully, predict how many litres of water will flow from hose B in 50 seconds. _____

Venn diagrams

At a ballet school, some girls do jazz only, some do ballet only, and some do both. First study the example carefully, then in each problem use the information to complete the diagram and answer the question.

In the class of 20 girls, 16 girls do jazz and 9 do both jazz and ballet.
How many girls do only ballet? _____

Note that in the circle for jazz there are 16 girls.
Since there are 20 girls there will be 4 who do ballet only.

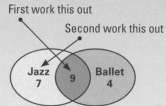

First work this out
Second work this out

Jazz 7 — 9 — Ballet 4

1 In the class of 20 girls, 13 girls do jazz and 5 girls do both jazz and ballet. How many girls do only ballet?

_____

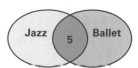

Jazz 5 Ballet

2 In the class of 25 girls, 14 girls do only jazz and 8 girls do only ballet. How many girls do both jazz and ballet?

_____

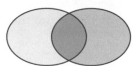

3 In the class of 24 girls, 19 girls do jazz and 8 girls do only ballet. How many girls do both jazz and ballet?

_____

4 In the class of 24 students, 19 students do jazz and 12 students do ballet.

a How many students do both jazz and ballet? _____

b If a person is selected at random, what is the probability that the student picked:

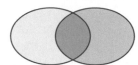

    i does only ballet? _____

    ii does only jazz? _____

    iii does not do both jazz and ballet? _____

5 120 students were surveyed as to whether they do jazz and/or ballet.
60% of those surveyed did jazz.
40% of those surveyed did both jazz and ballet.
75% of those who did ballet also did jazz.

Number of students who do neither

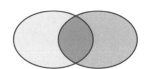

a Complete all the numbers in this Venn diagram.

b What is the probability that a student selected at random from the 120 surveyed:

    i does ballet? _____

    ii does not do jazz or ballet? _____

36

Chance & Data

Odd one out

Colour in the bubble next to the answer.

1 ◯ $20.05   ◯ $20 and 5 cents   ◯ 205 cents   ◯ 2005 cents

2 ◯ $4 and 30c   ◯ $4.30   ◯ 430c   ◯ 403c

3 ◯ 30c   ◯ $0.30   ◯ 20c + 5c + 5c   ◯ $3.00 ÷ 100

4 ◯ 1 L 45 mL   ◯ 1·405 L   ◯ 1 L 405 mL   ◯ 1405 mL

5 ◯ 500 mL   ◯ half a litre   ◯ 0·5 L   ◯ 5000 mL

6 ◯ 5080 mL   ◯ 5·8 L   ◯ 5·08 L   ◯ 5 L 80 mL

7 ◯ 0·131 m   ◯ 131 cm   ◯ 1·31 m   ◯ 1 m 31 cm

8 ◯ 852 mm   ◯ 0·852 m   ◯ 85·2 cm   ◯ 8·52 cm

9 ◯ 10 km 10 m   ◯ 10·01 km   ◯ 10·001 km   ◯ 10010 m

10 ◯ quarter of a metre   ◯ 2500 mm   ◯ 25 cm   ◯ 250 mm

11 ◯ 38·5 mm   ◯ 3·85 cm   ◯ 0·0385 m   ◯ 0·385 cm

12 ◯ 0·26 km   ◯ 2600 m   ◯ 2·6 km   ◯ 260 000 cm

13 ◯ 2540 g   ◯ 0·254 kg   ◯ 2 kg 540 g   ◯ 2·54 kg

14 ◯ 750 g   ◯ 0·075 kg   ◯ $\frac{3}{4}$ kg   ◯ 0·75 kg

15 ◯ 5:30   ◯ five-thirty   ◯ thirty minutes to 5   ◯ half-past five

16 ◯ 10:11 p.m.   ◯ 10 to 11 p.m.   ◯ 10:50 p.m.   ◯ 10-fifty p.m.

17 ◯ 1 min. 20 sec.   ◯ 62 sec.   ◯ 80 sec.   ◯ $1\frac{1}{3}$ min.

18 ◯ 104 hours   ◯ 52 hours   ◯ $2\frac{1}{6}$ day   ◯ 2 days 4 hours

Time zones

When it is early morning in London, it is late evening in Sydney.

All over the world, time zones are fixed according to the time at Greenwich, in London.

This map and the table on the opposite page show the time in various parts of the world when it is 12 midnight (Sunday/Monday) in London. Places east of Greenwich are ahead of it in time, whereas those places west of Greenwich are behind it in time. The International Date Line, drawn to follow approximately the 180° meridian, differs in time from Greenwich by 12 hours.

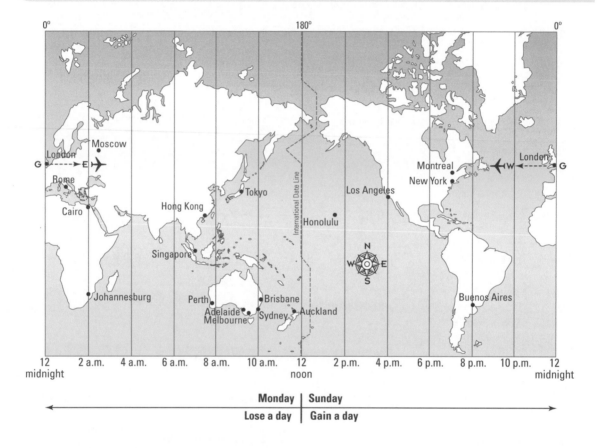

Complete the following statements.

Example: Sydney is **10** hours **ahead of** Greenwich.

1 Hong Kong is _____ hours _____ Greenwich.

2 Honolulu is _____ hours _____ Greenwich.

3 New York is _____ hours _____ Greenwich.

4 Tokyo is _____ hours _____ Greenwich.

5 Tokyo is _____ hours _____ New York.

6 London is _____ hours _____ Los Angeles.

7 Auckland is _____ hours _____ Perth.

8 Honolulu is _____ hours _____ Tokyo.

World times

Refer to the map on the previous page and the following table to answer these questions.

1 If it is 5 p.m. on Tuesday in Melbourne, what is the time in these cities?

   a Adelaide _____

   b Brisbane _____

   c London _____

   d Perth _____

   e Singapore _____

   f Auckland _____

   g Hong Kong _____

   h Rome _____

   i Moscow _____

2 If it is noon on Monday in New York, what time is it in these places?

   a Los Angeles _____

   b Montreal _____

   c Buenos Aires _____

   d Honolulu _____

   e Tokyo _____

   f Sydney _____

   g Perth _____

   h Moscow _____

   i Cairo _____

City	Time	Day
London	12 midnight	Sunday/Monday
Rome	1:00 a.m.	Monday
Cairo	2:00 a.m.	Monday
Johannesburg	2:00 a.m.	Monday
Moscow	3:00 a.m.	Monday
Singapore	7:30 a.m.	Monday
Hong Kong	8:00 a.m.	Monday
Perth	8:00 a.m.	Monday
Tokyo	9:00 a.m.	Monday
Adelaide	9:30 a.m.	Monday
Sydney	10:00 a.m.	Monday
Melbourne	10:00 a.m.	Monday
Brisbane	10:00 a.m.	Monday
Auckland	12:00 noon	Monday
Honolulu	2:00 p.m.	Sunday
Los Angeles	4:00 p.m.	Sunday
New York	7:00 p.m.	Sunday
Montreal	7:00 p.m.	Sunday
Buenos Aires	8:00 p.m.	Sunday

3 I would like to phone a friend in London and want the phone to ring there at 8 p.m. At what time should I phone from Brisbane? _____

4 My cousin in London wants to phone me in Sydney for my birthday. He wants the phone to ring at 7 a.m. Sydney time. At what time in London should he ring? _____

Mass puzzles

1 At the local market, Mr Obsolete uses a balance scale to weigh his carrots. He has three 3 kg masses and three 5 kg masses. With these he can weigh 1 kg of carrots, as shown in the illustration. Complete this table, showing how Mr Obsolete can weigh every whole-number amount from 2 kg to 16 kg with his six masses.

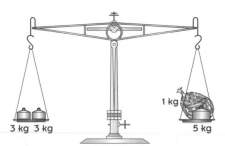

Left side	Right side	
Mass	Mass	Carrots
3 kg + 3 kg	5 kg	1 kg
		2 kg
		3 kg
		4 kg
		5 kg
		6 kg
		7 kg
		8 kg
		9 kg
		10 kg
		11 kg
		12 kg
		13 kg
		14 kg
		15 kg
		16 kg

2 Joe Obsolete sells other vegetables at a stall next to his father's. With his balance scale he uses only 5 kg and 8 kg masses.

Draw up a table similar to that above to show how Joe would weigh every whole-number amount from 1 kg to 6 kg. You can see how Joe would weigh 7 kg on the balance scale below.

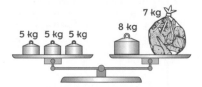

3 A box with 10 marbles in it has a mass of 84 g. The same box with 5 marbles in it has a mass of 54 g.

What is the mass of the box? _____

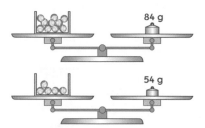

4 On a scale, a full sack of potatoes exactly balances half a sack of potatoes together with a 6 kg mass.

How heavy is a full sack of potatoes? _____

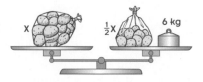

5 On a scale, three full sacks of apples exactly balance half a sack of apples together with a 10 kg mass.

How heavy is a full sack of apples? _____

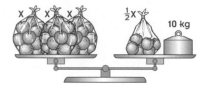

Fractions and measurement

1 Gaby had 30 minutes left to complete an examination. How long was the examination:

    a if this was $\frac{1}{3}$ of the total time? _____

    b if this was $\frac{2}{3}$ of the total time? _____

    c if this was $\frac{3}{4}$ of the total time? _____

    d if this was $\frac{3}{8}$ of the total time? _____

2 How many packets of nuts each with a mass of:

    a $\frac{3}{4}$ kg can be packed from a 12 kg container? _____

    b $\frac{2}{3}$ kg can be packed from a 12 kg container? _____

3 After the Ho family had eaten $\frac{3}{8}$ of the fruit they bought, there was 1·5 kg of it left. What was the original mass of fruit they bought? _____

4 Alex's mass is exactly half of his father's mass. If Alex and his father together have a mass of 120 kg, what is Alex's mass?

    _____

5 Mrs Lee and her daughter Faye have a mass of 105 kg. Faye's mass is $\frac{3}{4}$ of her mother's mass. What is Faye's mass? _____

6 A tank is $\frac{1}{4}$ full. After 20 L were added, it was $\frac{1}{3}$ full. What was the capacity of the tank? _____

7 A case $\frac{1}{2}$ full of apples has a mass of 10 kg. The same case $\frac{2}{3}$ full of apples has a mass of 13 kg. What is the mass of the empty case? _____

8 A case $\frac{1}{2}$ full of pears has a mass of 18 kg. The same case $\frac{1}{3}$ full of pears has a mass of 13 kg. What is the mass of the empty case? _____

Measuring with fractions

1 How long would it take to swim two lengths of a 50 m pool if the swimmer could cover $1\frac{1}{4}$ m in a second? _____

2 The width of a rectangle is $\frac{3}{4}$ of its length.
If the perimeter is 70 cm, find its length _____ and width _____.

3 The perimeter of a triangle is 26 cm. The shortest side is $\frac{1}{2}$ of the longest side, while the third side is $\frac{2}{3}$ of the longest side.
Find the length of each side (sides are whole numbers). _____

4 The petrol tank of a car with capacity of 64 L is $\frac{3}{4}$ filled. If $\frac{1}{3}$ of the fuel is used up during a trip, how much petrol is needed to completely fill the tank?

_____

5 James drank $\frac{1}{3}$ of a container of juice. He spilled $\frac{1}{4}$ of the remainder, and drank the last 120 mL. How much was in the container at first? _____

6 Paul drank $\frac{3}{4}$ of a container of juice and found that half of the remainder was 60 mL. How much was in the container at first? _____

$\frac{3}{4}$ drank

7 The total mass of a truck and its load is 2964 kg.
After delivering half the load, the mass of the truck and the remaining half-load is 2712 kg. What was the mass of the full load? _____

8 While at camp, I spent $\frac{1}{3}$ of my time sleeping, and $\frac{1}{4}$ of the remaining time I spent playing sport.
If I spent 24 hours on other activities, how long was the camp? _____

$\frac{1}{3}$ sleeping

9 Julian's dad drove him to the train station, $\frac{1}{3}$ of the way to school.
Julian then travelled $\frac{3}{4}$ of his remaining journey by train, and the rest of the trip of 2 km by the school bus. How far does Julian live from school?

_____

$\frac{1}{3}$ drove

enrich-e-matics
3rd EDITION
BOOK 6
ANSWERS

Missing numbers (page 1)

1 Rule: +5 ×4 −8 ÷2   **2** Rule: +5 ×4 −8 ÷2
3 15, 60, 52   **4** 16, 64, 56, 28   **5** 7, 48, 40, 20
6 6, 11, 36, 18   **7** 3, 8, 32, 12   **8** 4, 9, 36, 14
9 2, 7, 28, 20   **10** 15, 20, 80, 72   **11** 0, 5, 20, 12
12 $\frac{1}{2}$, $5\frac{1}{2}$ or $\frac{11}{2}$, 22, 14   **13** $\frac{3}{4}$, $5\frac{3}{4}$ or $\frac{23}{4}$, 23, 15
14 $\frac{1}{4}$, $5\frac{1}{4}$ or $\frac{21}{4}$, 21, 13

Secret rules (page 2)

1 17, 13, 7, 19, 23 (× 2 − 3)
2 10, 5, 82, 122, 65   (square + 1)
3 37, 52, 17, 47, 57 (× 5 + 2)
4 10, 28, 13, 16, 34   (× 3 − 2)
5 13, 9, 15, 7, 17   (× 2 + 5)
6 16, 4, 49, 36, 81   (− 1 then square)
7 71, 53, 35, 98, 8   (× 9 − 1)
8 14, 10, 8, 24, 22   (+ 2 then double)
9 9, 0, 3, 27, 18   (− 1 × 3)
10 12, 0, 2, 90, 132   (× by number before)

Square puzzles (page 3)

1 A = 5, B = 3, C = 2, D = 1   **2** B = 3, C = 1, D = 2, E = 4
3 A = 2, B = 3, C = 5, D = 1   **4** A = 2, B = 5, C = 4, D = 3
5 B = 2, C = 1, D = 5, E = 3

Find three numbers (page 4)

1 5, 10, 9   **2** 8, 11, 1   **3** 6, 12, 9
4 12, 4, 8   **5** 24, 4, 6   **6** 24, 8, 3
7 36, 4, 6   **8** 36, 9, 4   **9** 4, 5, 20
10 27, 3, 8

What's my pattern? (page 5)

There are other solutions.
1 27, 81, 243 (× 3)   11, 17, 19 (+ 2, + 6)
27, 33, 99 (× 3, + 6)   11, 33, 35 (+ 2, × 3)
2 9, 14, 23 (each term the sum of the two previous terms)
20, 21, 84 (× 4, + 1)   12, 13, 28 (× 2, + 2, + 1)
3 10, 15, 21 (triangular numbers, or differences increasing by 1)
8, 11, 13 (+ 2, + 3)   18, 36, 108 (× 3, × 2)
4 8, 12, 17 (differences increasing by 1)
6, 8, 9 (+ 1, + 2)   7, 11, 13 (prime numbers)
5 3, 5, 8 (each term the sum of the two previous terms)
2, 4, 4 (× 1, × 2)   4, 7, 11 (differences increasing by 1)
6 16, 25, 36 (differences increasing by 2, or square numbers)
12, 17, 20 (+ 3, + 5)   36, 41, 164 (× 4, + 5)

7 8, 10, 12 (+ 2)   12, 14, 28 (× 2, + 2)
10, 16, 26 (each term the sum of the two previous terms)
8 9, 13, 18, (differences increasing by 1)
7, 9, 10 (+ 1, + 2)   10, 18, 34 (× 2 then − 2)
9 2, $2\frac{1}{2}$, 3 (+ $\frac{1}{2}$)   3, $3\frac{1}{2}$, 7 (× 2, + $\frac{1}{2}$)
$2\frac{1}{2}$, 4, $6\frac{1}{2}$ (each term the sum of the two previous terms)
10 11, 20, 21 (+ 1, + 9)   11, 110, 111 (+ 1, × 10)
11, 100, 101 (binary numbers: 0, 1, 1, 2, 3, 4, 5, …)
11 24, 48, 96 (× 2)   15, 30, 33 (+ 3, × 2)
24, 30, 60 (× 2, + 6)
12 125, 625, 3125 (× 5)   29, 145, 149 (+ 4, × 5)
125, 145, 725 (× 5, + 20)   29, 49, 53 (+ 4, + 20)

Magic squares (page 6)

1 a
$2\frac{1}{2}$	2	$4\frac{1}{2}$
5	3	1
$1\frac{1}{2}$	4	$3\frac{1}{2}$

9

b
$1\frac{1}{4}$	$1\frac{1}{2}$	$\frac{1}{4}$
0	1	2
$1\frac{3}{4}$	$\frac{1}{2}$	$\frac{3}{4}$

3

c
$\frac{1}{3}$	$2\frac{2}{3}$	1
2	$1\frac{1}{3}$	$\frac{2}{3}$
$1\frac{2}{3}$	0	$2\frac{1}{3}$

4

d
1	$\frac{4}{5}$	$1\frac{4}{5}$
2	$1\frac{1}{5}$	$\frac{2}{5}$
$\frac{3}{5}$	$1\frac{3}{5}$	$1\frac{2}{5}$

$3\frac{3}{5}$

e
$1\frac{1}{2}$	$1\frac{1}{4}$	$2\frac{1}{2}$
$2\frac{3}{4}$	$1\frac{3}{4}$	$\frac{3}{4}$
1	$2\frac{1}{4}$	2

$5\frac{1}{4}$

f
0.6	0.7	0.2
0.1	0.5	0.9
0.8	0.3	0.4

1.5

g
0.7	0.8	0.3
0.2	0.6	1
0.9	0.4	0.5

1.8

h
0.8	0.7	1.2
1.3	0.9	0.5
0.6	1.1	1

2.7

2 a 2·4, 2·8   **b** 3·5, 4   **c** 3·7, 3·8   **d** 3·25, 4·25
e 2, 2·5   **f** 2, 4·5   **g** 1, 5·5   **h** 6·4, 0·1
i 2, 2·2   **j** 4, 0·2

Decimal challenges (page 7)

1 C   **2** B   **3** A   **4** D   **5** E   **6** E
7 C   **8** A   **9** B   **10** A   **11** C   **12** E

True or false? (page 8)

1 T   **2** F   **3** T   **4** F   **5** F   **6** F   **7** T
8 F   **9** F   **10** F   **11** T   **12** T   **13** T   **14** T
15 T   **16** T   **17** T   **18** T   **19** T   **20** T   **21** F
22 T   **23** F   **24** T   **25** T   **26** T   **27** T   **28** T
29 F   **30** T   **31** T   **32** T   **33** T   **34** T   **35** T
36 T   **37** T   **38** T   **39** T   **40** T   **41** F   **42** T
43 F   **44** F   **45** T   **46** F   **47** T   **48** F   **49** T
50 T   **51** T   **52** T   **53** T   **54** F   **55** F   **56** T
57 T   **58** T   **59** F   **60** T

Fraction fun (page 9)

1 20   **2** $\frac{1}{2}$ **3** 12   **4** $\frac{1}{5}$ **5** 50   **6** $\frac{1}{5}$
7 $\frac{1}{6}$ **8** 36   **9** 25   **10** 16   **11** 24   **12** $\frac{1}{4}$
13 $\frac{1}{3}$ **14** $\frac{1}{2}$ **15** $\frac{1}{3}$ **16** 8   **17** 27   **18** 40

5 Daisy spoke for 30 min., the longest time for the least cost, so her call was likely to be local—or at least nearer than Margaret's or Eva's. Eva called the longest distance— a 10 min. call cost her the most. Margaret's call was further than Daisy's but not as far as Eva's.

Graphs (page 35)

1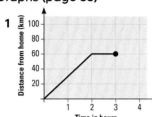

2 a A

b C and D are the same age. However, C is also taller than D. A and C are the same height. However, A is younger than C.

3 a 150 L   **b** 10 seconds   **c** 120 L   **d** 450 L

Venn diagrams (page 36)

1 7   **2** 3   **3** 3

4 a 7   **b i** $\frac{5}{24}$ **ii** $\frac{12}{24} = \frac{1}{2}$ **iii** $\frac{17}{24}$

5 a

b i $\frac{64}{120} = \frac{8}{15}$ **ii** $\frac{32}{120} = \frac{4}{15}$

Odd one out (page 37)

1 205 cents   **2** 403c   **3** $3.00 ÷100   **4** 1 L 45 mL
5 5000 mL   **6** 5·8 L   **7** 0·131 m   **8** 8·52 cm
9 10·001 km   **10** 2500 mm   **11** 0·385 cm   **12** 0·26 km
13 0·254 kg   **14** 0·075 kg   **15** thirty minutes to 5
16 10:11 p.m.   **17** 62 sec.   **18** 104 hours

Time zones (page 38)

1 8 ahead   **2** 10 behind   **3** 5 behind   **4** 9 ahead
5 14 ahead   **6** 8 ahead   **7** 4 ahead   **8** 19 behind

World times (page 39)

1 a 4:30 p.m. Tuesday   **b** 5 p.m. Tuesday   **c** 7 a.m. Tuesday
d 3 p.m. Tuesday   **e** 2:30 p.m. Tuesday   **f** 7 p.m. Tuesday
g 3 p.m. Tuesday   **h** 8 a.m. Tuesday   **i** 10 a.m. Tuesday
2 a 9 a.m. Monday   **b** 12 noon Monday   **c** 1 p.m. Monday
d 7 a.m. Monday   **e** 2 a.m. Tuesday   **f** 3 a.m. Tuesday
g 1 a.m. Tuesday   **h** 8 p.m. Monday   **i** 7 p.m. Monday
3 6 a.m next day   **4** 9 p.m. previous day

Mass puzzles (page 40)

1

3 + 3	5	1
5	3	2
3		3
3 + 3 + 3 or 5 + 5	5 or 3 + 3	4
5		5
3 + 3		6
5 + 5	3	7
5 + 3		8
3 + 3 + 3		9
5 + 5		10
5 + 3 + 3		11
5 + 5 + 5	3	12
5 + 5 + 3		13
5 + 3 + 3 + 3		14
5 + 5 + 5		15
5 + 5 + 3 + 3		16

2

Left side	Right side	
Mass kg	**Mass kg**	**Carrots kg**
8 + 8	5 + 5 + 5	1
5 + 5	8	2
8	5	3
8 + 8 + 8	5 + 5 + 5 + 5	4
5		5
8 + 8	5 + 5	6

3 24 g
4 12 kg
5 4 kg

Fractions and measurement (page 41)

1 a 90 min.   **b** 45 min.   **c** 40 min.   **d** 80 min.
2 a 16   **b** 18   **3** 4 kg   **4** 40 kg
5 45 kg   **6** 240 L   **7** 1 kg   **8** 3 kg

Measuring with fractions (page 42)

1 80 sec. = 1 min. 20 sec.   **2** 15 cm
3 6 cm, 8 cm, 12 cm   **4** 32 L   **5** 240 mL
6 480 mL   **7** 504 kg   **8** 48 hours   **9** 12 km

Perimeter and area (page 43)

1 24 cm, 6 cm   **2** 36 cm²   **3** 32 cm
4 13 cm   **5** 40 cm²
6 a 3 cm, 6 cm, 6 cm   **b** 7 cm, 14 cm, 14 cm
7 a 80 cm²   **b** 36 cm   **c** 960 cm
8 a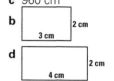

Perimeter challenges (page 44)

1 32 cm   **2** 24 cm   **3** 3 m x 9 m and $4\frac{1}{2}$ x 6 m
4 a 8 cm   **b** 10 cm   **5 a i** 14 cm   **ii** 16 cm   **b** 8

Area challenges (page 45)

1 110   **2** 450   **3 a** 98 cm   **b** 54 cm²
4 a 324 cm²   **b** B = 81 cm² C = 100 cm²   D = 49 cm²
   E = 225 cm²   F = 16 cm²   G = 196 cm²
5 10 cm   **6** 190 cm
7 a l = 4 cm, w = 3 cm, h = 2 cm
b l = 9 cm, w = 3 cm, h = 4 cm

Paving stones (page 46)

1 a 12, 16, 20   **b** 44
   c Number of paving stones = 4 x (length of side of garden + 1)
      Number of paving stones = 4 x length of side of garden + 4
d 124   **e** 20
2 a 52 m²   **b** 52   **c** 38
3 60 black, 180 brown

Area explorations (page 47)

1

L (m)	B (m)	A (m²)		L (m)	B (m)	A (m²)
46	1	46		26	11	286
44	2	88		*24	12	288
42	3	126		22	13	286
40	4	160		20	14	280
38	5	190		18	15	270
36	6	216		16	16	256
34	7	238		14	17	238
32	8	256		12	18	216
30	9	270		10	19	190
28	10	280		*largest area		

2 a 5 cm   **b** 13 cm   **c** 10 cm   **3** 33 cm²

Cough medicine (page 48)

1 a 4 times   **b** 20 mL   **c** 40   **d** 10 days
2 a 5 times   **b** 50 mL   **c** 20   **d** 4 days
   e Tuesday 11 p.m.
3 a 5 times   **b** 12·5 mL   **c** 80   **d** 16 days
   e Sunday 10 p.m.

Volume & surface area (page 49)

1

Total edge length (cm)	12	24	36	48	60	72
Surface area (cm²)	6	24	54	96	150	216
Volume (cm³)	1	8	27	64	125	216

D

Tessa's world trip (page 24)

1 a £320   **b** A$200   **c** $280

2 a 240 Euros   **b** A$60   **c** A$200

3 a 1800 kronor   **b** A$40   **c** A$250

4 a 30000 forints   **b** A$66

5 a 6000 rupees   **b** A$12.50

6 a A$1.33   **b** US$600   **c** A$80

   d US$360   **e** A$400

Hiring a bus (page 25)

1 a $300   **b** $12   **c** $280   **d** $340

2 a $275   **b** $11   **c** $225   **d** $375

3 a $275   **b** $495

4 a Both are the same price.   **b & c** Friendly bus company

Matchstick puzzles (page 26)

1 6, 9, 12, 15, → 30   The number of matches required is 3 times the number on each side of a triangle.

2 6, 12, 20, 30, → 110   The number of matches required is the number of L's times the next highest number.

3 10, 18, 28, 40, → 130   The number of matches required is the number of the step times the number 3 more than the height.

4 10, 14, 18, 22, → 44   The number of matches required is 4 times the number of hexagons plus 2.

5 10, 16, 22, 28, → 58   The number of matches required is 6 times the number of diamonds, less 2.

6 12, 19, 26, 33, → 68   The number of matches required is 2 less than 7 times the number of pentagons.

Patterns with squares (page 27)

1 9; 11, 13   **2** 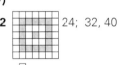 24; 32, 40

3  28; 36, 44   **4** 7; 9, 11

Counting techniques (page 28)

1 a 6   **b** 9

2 a 12   **b** 3   **c** 24   **d** 6   **e** 18   **f** 24

   g 6   **h** 18   **i** 6   **j** 4   **k** 12

3 a 8   **4 a** 16   **b** 36

Number plates (page 29)

1 100   **2** 1000

3 a 26   **b** 26   **c** 100   **d** 100   **e** 10   **f** 2600

4 a 26   **b** 676   **c** 100   **d** 676 000

5 a 676   **b** 17 576   **c** 1000   **d** 17 576 000

Listing possibilities (page 30)

1 10   **2** 12

3 brown/egg, brown/cheese, brown/tuna, brown/honey, white/egg, white/cheese, white/tuna, white/honey

4 a 3   **b** 6   **c** 10   **d** 15   **e** 45

5 a 6   **b** 12   **c** 20   **d** 380

6 a 2   **b i** 5   **ii** 4   **iii** 3   **iv** 2   **v** 1

Possibilities (page 31)

1

50c	20c	10c	5c
1	1	1	4
1		4	2
	4	1	2
	3		4

2 31 possibilities

$1	50c	20c	10c
1	1	1	3
1	1	2	1
1		5	
1	4	4	2
1		3	4
1		2	6
1		1	8
	3	1	3
	3	2	1
	2	5	0
	2	4	2
	2	3	4
	2	2	6
	2	1	8
	1	7	1
	1	6	3
	1	5	5
	1	4	7
	1	3	9
	1	2	11
	1	1	13
		10	
		9	2
		8	4
		7	6
		6	8
		5	10
		4	12
		3	14
		2	16
		1	18

3 a 28   **b** 7   **c** 168

4 63

5 a 69   **b** 104

6 a 39   **b** 99

7 a 81   **b** 41   **c** 40   **d** 72

8 a 8   **b** 12

What's the chance? (page 32)

1 a 64   **b** 2   **c** 16

   d i $\frac{1}{64}$ **ii** $\frac{3}{64}$ **iii** $\frac{8}{64} = \frac{1}{8}$

   e 2 and 16, 3 and 15, 4 and 14, 5 and 13, 6 and 12, 7 and 11, 8 and 10

2 a i a $\frac{1}{4}$, b $\frac{1}{2}$, c $\frac{1}{8}$, d $\frac{3}{4}$

   ii a $\frac{5}{12}$, b $\frac{1}{12}$, c $\frac{1}{4}$, d $\frac{1}{2}$

   iii a $\frac{1}{4}$, b $\frac{1}{6}$, c $\frac{1}{6}$, d $\frac{5}{12}$.

   iv a $\frac{1}{4}$, b $\frac{1}{8}$, c $\frac{1}{2}$, d $\frac{3}{8}$

   v a $\frac{1}{5}$, b $\frac{2}{5}$, c $\frac{1}{5}$, d $\frac{3}{5}$

Chance and data (page 33)

1 a A person turns on the tap for 5 minutes, filling the bathtub to a height of about 15 cm. He then sits in the bath, raising the water level by another 5 cm. He relaxes in the bath for 5 minutes before turning the tap on again for about 5 minutes to raise the level to 40 cm, with him in the bathtub. The person then relaxed in the bathtub for another 5 minutes before getting out of the bath and pulling out the plug. The water takes 5 minutes to drain from the bath.

b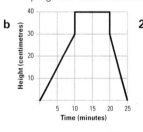

2 a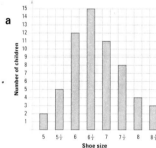

b 60   **c** $\frac{12}{60} = \frac{1}{5}$

d 20%   **e** $\frac{15}{60} = \frac{1}{4}$ or 25%

f 25%   **g** $\frac{5}{60} = \frac{1}{12} = 8\frac{1}{3}$ %

Interpreting graphs (page 34)

1 a Marc   **b** Bob

2 1: George   2: Claire   3: Faye   4: Tim   5: Marc

3 a 1: Jessica   2: Alice   3: Doug   4: Monica   5: Harry

   b 1: Jessica   2: Alice   3: Harry   4: Monica   5: Doug

   c 1: Jessica   2: Alice   3: Harry   4: Monica   5: Doug

4 a A person travels at the same speed for 2 hours, stays in one place (possibly resting) for an hour, then returns at a slower speed taking 3 hours.

   b A person travels 10 km in 10 minutes (60 km/h), then travels 20 km in 10 min., which is 120 km/h.

19 16   **20** 20   **21** 2   **22** 3   **23** 2   **24** 3
25 3   **26** 100   **27** 40   **28** 10   **29** 4   **30** 10

Fraction challenges (page 10)

1 a 16   **b** 32   **c** 16   **d** 27   **e** 49
f 100   **g** 50   **h** 18   **i** 10   **j** 16
k 12   **l**   **m** $\frac{3}{4}$ **n** $\frac{1}{3}$ **o** $\frac{1}{2}$

2 $\frac{3}{4}$, $\frac{1}{4}$ **3** $\frac{2}{3}$, $\frac{1}{3}$ **4** $\frac{3}{2}$, $\frac{1}{2}$

5 Any fraction greater than 1 (e.g. $\frac{3}{2}$, since $(\frac{3}{2})^2 > \frac{3}{2}$)...

6 Any fraction smaller than 1 and greater than 0 (e.g. $\frac{1}{2}$ or $\frac{3}{4}$),
since $(\frac{1}{2})^2 < \frac{1}{2}$ $(\frac{1}{4} < \frac{1}{2})$ and $(\frac{3}{4})^2 < \frac{3}{4}$ $(\frac{9}{16} < \frac{3}{4})$

7 a $\frac{1}{2} + \frac{1}{8}$ **b** $\frac{1}{2} + \frac{1}{10}$ **c** $\frac{1}{2} + \frac{1}{3}$ **d** $\frac{1}{2} + \frac{1}{5}$
e $\frac{1}{2} + \frac{1}{12}$ or $\frac{1}{3} + \frac{1}{4}$ **f** $\frac{1}{2} + \frac{1}{6} + \frac{1}{15}$

Find the fraction (page 11)

1 a ☐ = 4   **b** ★ = 6   **c** ◯ = 6   **d** ◇ = 9
e # = 12   **f** ◯ = 8   **g** ▯ = 3   **h** ⬠ = 5
i ⊙ = 5, ⊡ = 2   **j** ◯ = 4, ◼ = 7

2 a $\frac{5}{12}$ **b** $\frac{1}{3}$ **3 a** $\frac{3}{2}$ **b** $\frac{9}{4}$ **c** $\frac{4}{3}$

4 a $\frac{1}{3}$ **b** $\frac{1}{5}$ **c** $\frac{3}{5}$ **d** $\frac{2}{3}$ **e** $\frac{3}{5}$ **f** $\frac{2}{5}$ **g** $\frac{5}{12}$ **h** $\frac{3}{7}$

5 a $\frac{4}{5}$, $\frac{5}{6}$, $\boxed{\frac{6}{7}}$, $\boxed{\frac{1}{2}}$ **b** 2, $\frac{7}{4}$, $\boxed{\frac{8}{5}}$, $\boxed{4}$ **c** $\frac{4}{9}$, $\frac{1}{2}$, $\boxed{\frac{3}{4}}$, $\boxed{\frac{1}{6}}$

Spending money (page 12)

1 a $48   **b** $72   **c** $36   **d** $48   **e** $72
2 a $8   **b** $48   **3 a** $10   **b** $80

Consecutive numbers (page 13)

1 a 11, 12   **b** 8, 9, 10   **c** 6, 7   **d** 3, 4, 5
e 16, 18, 20   **f** 19, 21   **g** 24, 25, 26   **h** 23, 25, 27

2 a No (the sum of an even and an odd number is always odd).
b Yes (an even number times an odd number is always even).
c Yes (one of the numbers will always be a multiple of 3).
d Yes (from **c**, above, the product is always divisible by 3;
and **b**, the product will be divisible by 2 and 3, which is 6).

3 Always 1   **4 a, b**   For both. Result will always be 4

Factorial notation (page 14)

1 a 5   **b** 6   **c** 7   **d** 10
e 20   **f** 20   **g** 30   **h** 90
2 a 4!   **b** 7!   **c** 9!   **d** 8!   **e** 7!
f 10!   **g** 9!   **h** 18!   **i** 17!   **j** 16!

3 $1 \times 1! + 2 \times 2! + 3 \times 3! + 4 \times 4! = 5! - 1$
$1 \times 1! + 2 \times 2! + 3 \times 3! + 4 \times 4! + 5 \times 5! = 6! - 1$

Four 4s problem (page 15)

Some calculations that have been useful:

$\sqrt{.4} = \sqrt{\frac{4}{9}} = \frac{2}{3}$ $4! \times \sqrt{.4} = 24 \times \frac{2}{3} = 16$

$4! \div \sqrt{.4} = 24 \times \frac{3}{2} = 36$ $4! \div \sqrt{.4} = 4 \times \frac{3}{2} = 6$

$\frac{4 - .4}{.4} = \frac{40 - 4}{4} = 9$ $\frac{4! - \sqrt{4}}{.4} = 22 \times \frac{10}{4} = 55$

$\frac{4!}{.4 \times .4} = 24 \times \frac{10}{4} \times \frac{10}{4} = 150$ $\frac{4!}{.4 \times \sqrt{.4}} = 24 \times \frac{9}{4} \times \frac{3}{2} = 81$

$\frac{4! + .4}{.4} = \frac{240 + 4}{4} = 61$ $\frac{4 \times 4}{.4 \times .4} = 16 \times \frac{9}{4} \times \frac{10}{4} = 90$

Sequences (page 16)

1 a 35, 74   **b** 58, 148   **c** 85, 295   **d** 65, 184
e 92, 272   **f** 43, 167   **g** 147, 97   **h** 135, 83
i 16, 128   **j** 27, 243

2 a 2, 4, 6, 8, 10   **b** 1, 4, 7, 10, 13   **c** 3, 5, 7, 9, 11
d 2, 7, 12, 17, 22   **e** 2, 6, 10, 14, 18   **f** 3, 10, 17, 24, 31
g 2, 8, 14, 20, 26   **h** 1, 9, 17, 25, 33
i 51, 47, 43, 39, 35   **j** 48, 43, 38, 33, 28

Bartering (page 17)

1 a 2   **b** 3   **c** 3   **d** 5   **e** 12
2 a 30   **b** 40   **c** 60
3 a 20   **b** 20   **c** 8   **d** 2   **e** 12
4 30 bananas or 15 oranges or 20 apples or 5 pineapples
5 42 bananas   **6** 9 pineapples   **7** 2 pineapples

Percentage challenges (page 18)

1 90   **2** 16   **3** 30   **4** 36   **5** 24
6 60   **7** 25   **8** 40   **9** 40   **10** 32
11 36   **12** 72   **13** 60   **14** 60   **15** 140
16 250   **17** 40   **18** 20   **19** 60   **20** $9600
21 $16 000   **22** $400

Percentage problems (page 19)

1 No; $150 – 20% = $120; $150 – 10% = $135 (Sale price);
$135 – 10% = $121.50 (Employee discount).
Actual discount equals 19% not 20%.
2 Cost is $92 in both cases.   **3** The dealer lost $1500.
4 Joseph's profit = $412.50   **5** Glenn paid $150.

Fruit arithmetic (page 20)

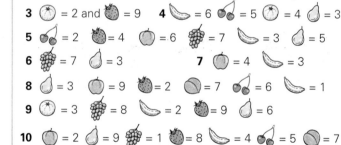

Divisibility number puzzles (page 21)

1 36   **2 a** 60   **b** 60   **c** 420   **d** 840
3 a 5   **b** 13   **c** 61   **d** 61
4 121   **5** 24   **6** 42 rabbits and 8 hutches
7 a B = 0 A = 3, 6 or 9 *or* B = 4, A = 2, 5 or 8
or B = 8, A = 1, 4 or 7
b A = 7 and B = 2   **8** 72

Money problems (page 22)

1 $60   **2** $120   **3 a** $6.90   **b** 17 words
4 a $64   **b** 35 kg< mass of parcel ≤ 40 kg
5 $750   **6** $8

Use your calculator (page 23)

1 $26 000   **2** $600   **3 a** $128   **b** $640
4 a $230   **b** $30   **5 a** $1080   **b** $230
6 a $740   **b** $742   **c** Nicky   **d** $2
7 a $6560   **b** $1560

Euler's formula (page 70)

1

Cube	6	8	12	2
Rectangular prism	6	8	12	2
Triangular prism	5	6	9	2
Square pyramid	5	5	8	2
Triangular pyramid	4	4	6	2

2 Euler proved that $F + V - E = 2$ for simple closed surfaces.

Locus (page 71)

1 **2** **3** **4**

5 a **b**

c **d**

What's my message? (page 72)

1 DO THE RIGHT THING   **2** I LOVE DANCING

Simpler problems first (page 73)

1 a 1   **b** 3   **c** 6   **d** 10   **e** 66
2 a 91   **b** 10
3 a 7, 8, 19, 49   **b i** 19   **ii** 49

Logic using scales (page 74)

1 9   **2** 2   **3** 3   **4** 2   **5** 3
6 7   **7** 6   **8** 13   **9** 4   **10** 1

Challenge on averages (page 75)

1 a 3   **b** 4   **c** 5   **d** 4   **e** 10   **f** 8
2 35 kg   **3** 7°C   **4** 12 kg   **5** 14 years
6 10°C   **7** 90 marks   **8** 54 kg

Working together (page 76)

1 9 days
2 John can paint $\frac{1}{3}$ room in 1 hour. Apprentice paints $\frac{1}{6}$ room in 1 hour. Together they paint $\frac{1}{3} + \frac{1}{6} = \frac{1}{2}$ room in 1 hr. Together they can paint 1 room in 2 hrs.
3 1 hr 12 min.   **4** 20 min.   **5** 1 day, 17 hrs, $8\frac{1}{2}$ min.

Counting frame mathematics (page 77)

1 a i 1152   **ii** 3012   **iii** 20421
b i 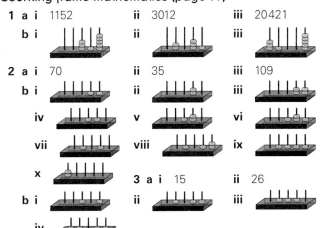   **ii**   **iii**

2 a i 70   **ii** 35   **iii** 109
b i   **ii**   **iii**
iv   **v**   **vi**
vii   **viii**   **ix**
x   **3 a i** 15   **ii** 26
b i   **ii**   **iii**
iv

Triangular numbers (page 78)

1 21, 28
2 15 21 28 36
      5   6   7   8   9
3 $1 + 2 + 3 + 4 + 5 + 6 = 21$ **4** $15 + 21 = 6^2$
$1 + 2 + 3 + 4 + 5 + 6 + 7 = 28$ $21 + 28 = 7^2$
$1 + 2 + 3 + 4 + 5 + 6 + 8 = 36$ $28 + 36 = 8^2$

If one triangular number is added to the next, the result is a square number.

5 $11 \times 11 - 1 = 120 = 8 \times 15$ **6** $8 \times 10 + 1 = 9^2$
$13 \times 13 - 1 = 168 = 8 \times 21$ $8 \times 15 + 1 = 11^2$
$8 \times 21 + 1 = 13^2$
$8 \times 28 + 1 = 15^2$

7 $19 = 3 + 6 + 10$ $21 = 6 + 15$ $29 = 28 + 1$
$35 = 28 + 6 + 1$ $36 =$ triangular number
$37 = 36 + 1$ $38 = 28 + 10$
$46 = 45 + 1$ or $36 + 10$ or $28 + 15 + 3$

Pascal's triangle (page 79)

1

4			1	4	6	4	1			$16 = 2^4$
5		1	5	10	10	5	1			$32 = 2^5$
6		1	6	15	20	15	6	1		$64 = 2^6$
7		1	7	21	35	35	21	7	1	$128 = 2^7$
8	1	8	28	56	70	56	28	8	1	$256 = 2^8$
9	1	9	36	84	126	126	84	36	9	1	$512 = 2^9$

2 121, 1331 and 14 641, which are the numbers in the second, third and fourth rows
3 a 6   **b** 9   **c** 15
4 a 3   **b** 6   **c** 10
d Triangular numbers   **e** 45
5 a 2, 3, 4, 5, 6, 7, …   **b** 3, 6, 10, 15, … (triangular numbers)
6 3, 6, 10, 15, … (again triangular numbers)
7 a 2, 4, 8, 16, 32, 64
b They are the powers of 2, and the powers are the same as the row numbers.
8 Third, seventh, eleventh, …
9 In every odd row, the middle numbers are the same; or the second and the second last numbers are always also the row number.

How many routes? (page 80)

1 a There are six paths from P to Q.

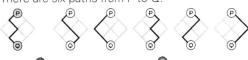

b 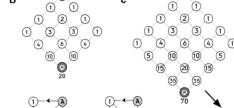 **c**

2 a 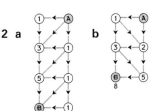 **b**

The symmetry figure diagram in **1 b** is embedded in this one; the numbers of paths follow the numbers in Pascal's triangle.

Polygons (page 63)

1

Sides of polygon	4	5	6	7	8
Number of triangles	2	3	4	5	6
Angle sum (degrees)	360°	540°	720°	900°	1080°

2 Angle sum of an 'n' sided polygon is (n − 2) × 180°, i.e. subtract 2 from the number of sides of the polygon and then multiply it by 180°

3 a 8 × 180° = 1440° **b** 10 × 180° = 1800°

What's my shape? (page 64)

1 a 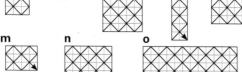 rhombus or ☐ square

b △ △ △ any isosceles triangle

c ☐ square or ▭ rectangle

d ☐ square, ▭ rectangle, ◇ rhombus or ▱ parallelogram

e ▭ rectangle or ☐ square

f ☐ square **g** ◯ circle

h △ isosceles triangle **i** ▽ equilateral triangle

j i ☐ square **ii** ◇ rhombus or ▭ rectangle

iii isosceles trapezium or kite

2 a cube **b** rectangular prism

c triangular pyramid (tetrahedron)

d triangular prism **e** sphere

f square pyramid **g** cylinder

h cone **i** square pyramid

j pentagonal pyramid

Billiards (page 65)

1 Note: the dimensions of figures p, q, r, s and t can be reduced.

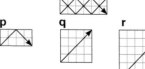
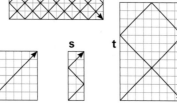

2 a upper right b upper left c lower right

d If the table is even by even, the dimensions can always be reduced, and the reduced form should be used to work out into which pocket the ball will fall.

3 The number of times the ball hits the side of the table will equal the sum of the length and the width, minus 2.

Cube explorations (page 66)

1 a 27 **b** 19 **c** 8

2 a 64 **b** 37 **c** 27

3

Size of cheese	Cubes cut	Cubes with wax	Cubes without wax
3 cm × 3 cm × 3 cm	27	26	1
4 cm × 4 cm × 4 cm	64	56	8
5 cm × 5 cm × 5 cm	125	98	27
6 cm × 6 cm × 6 cm	216	152	64
10 cm × 10 cm × 10 cm	1000	488	512
8 cm × 6 cm × 4 cm	192	144	48
7 cm × 5 cm × 4 cm	140	110	30

Experiments with cubes (page 67)

1 a 27 **b i** 8 **ii** 12 **iii** 6 **iv** 1

c 27. This is the same answer as for **a** above.

2 a 64 **b i** 8 **ii** 24 **iii** 24 **iv** 8

3 The following points can be noted:

- Irrespective of the size of a larger cube, the number of small cubes with paint on three faces is always 8.

- The total number of small cubes with paint on three faces, two faces, one face and none is equal to the total number that makes up the large one.

4 a 26 **b** 98 **5 a** 56 **b** 152

Curves from lines (page 68)

1
b
2 a
c

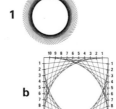
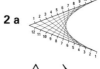

More curves (page 69)

1 a, b **2**

3 every point joined to 3 times itself

F

2 27 cm²   total surface area = 54 cm²
3 98 cm², 76 cm², 70 cm², 56 cm², 52 cm²,
4 a 2 cm   **b** 1728 cm³

Volume and capacity (page 50)

1 24   **2 a** 50   **b** 200   **c** 1000   **d** 10000
3 125   **4 a i** 8   **ii** 27   **b i** 3 cm   **ii** 2 cm
5 16 cm   **6** 432 g

Volume investigation (page 51)

Size of box (cm)	Volume of box (cm³)
1 × 8 × 8	64
2 × 6 × 6	72
3 × 4 × 4	48
4 × 2 × 2	16
1 × 10 × 10	100
2 × 8 × 8	128
3 × 6 × 6	108
4 × 4 × 4	64
5 × 2 × 2	20

Size of box (cm)	Volume of box (cm³)
1 × 12 × 12	144
2 × 10 × 10	200
3 × 8 × 8	192
4 × 6 × 6	144
5 × 4 × 4	80
6 × 2 × 2	24
1 × 13 × 13	169
2 × 11 × 11	242
3 × 9 × 9	243
4 × 7 × 7	196
5 × 5 × 5	125
6 × 3 × 3	54
7 × 1 × 1	7

Volume (page 52)

1 5 cm   **2 a** 3 cm
b 240 cm³   **3 a** 2 cm
b 140 cm³   **4** 15 cm
5 a 200 cm³   **b** 5 cm

Scale drawings (page 53)

1 a i 96 m   **ii** 48 m   **b i** 60 m   **ii** 100 m
2 a i 15 m   **ii** 30 cm or 0·3 m   **iii** 4.5 m
   b i 11 cm   **ii** 1·2 cm   **iii** 50 cm
3 7 cm   **4 a** 150 km   **b** 350 km   **5** 15 cm

Ratio problems (page 54)

1 a 60   **b** 200   **c** 240
2 a 6   **b** $20   **c** 24   **d** 16
3 a 8 m³ of metal; 3 m³ of sand; 1 m³ of cement
   b 20 m³ of metal; 15 m³ of sand; 5 m³ of cement
4 a 18 m   **b** 8 m   **c** 14 m
5 a 24 m   **b** 9 m
6 a i 648 km   **ii** 24 km   **iii** 96 km
   b i 3 L   **ii** 2 L   **iii** 9 L

Ratio and proportion (page 55)

1 a $8 and $16   **b** $6 and $18   **c** $4 and $20
2 a $20 and $40   **b** $15 and $45   **c** $12 and $48
3 12 parts metal; 9 parts sand; 6 parts cement
4 12   **5** Kumiko receives $4, Masika $8 and Inika $16
6 Gilah receives $1000, Jahinger $600 and Olga $400
7 6 children   **8** 21 metres

Rate problems (page 56)

1 15 kg   **2 a** 43   **b** 129   **c** 10 hours
3 25 minutes   **4** Dimitri $36, Lindsay $48
5 a 40   **b** 6 days   **6** 300
7 a 69c   **b** 9 minutes   **8 a** $321   **b** 350 km
9 a 300 km   **b** 15 km   **c** 40 L   **d** $12   **e** 1125 km

Dripping tap (page 57)

1 a 120 drops   **b** 24 mL
2 a 8 mL   **b** 480 mL   **c** 4·8 L   **d** 10 min.
   e 25 min.   **f** 10 hrs 25 min.

3 a 4 mL   **b** 1200 drops   **c** 5 drops
   d 0·2 mL   **e** 5·76 L
4 a 50 cm³   **b** 10 hours

Speed challenges (page 58)

1 a 90 000 m/h   **b** 1500 m/min.   **c** 25 m/sec.
   d 4 hrs   **e** 1 hr 20 min.   **f** 135 km
   g 15 km   **h** 1500 m
2 a 20 m   **b** 54 km/h
3 10 min. late   **4** 15 km/h   **5** 55 km/h
6 60 km/h   **7** after $2\frac{1}{2}$ hours

Speed problems (page 59)

1 2 hrs, 45 min.   **2 a** 12 min.   **b** 54 cm
3 a Michelle, by 5 minutes   **b** $2\frac{1}{2}$ minutes
4 a $1\frac{1}{2}$ hours after leaving home, between C and D
   b 2 hours after leaving home, between D and E
   c 40 km   **d** $13\frac{1}{3}$ km/h   **e** 5 km/h faster

Cutting rectangles (page 60)

1 9 cm × 2 cm   **2**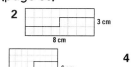

3 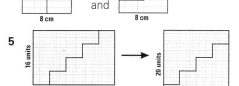   and   **4**

5 →

Solids (page 61)

1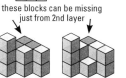

2

Nets (page 62)

1 a square pyramid   **b** triangular pyramid
   c triangular prism   **d** triangular prism

2

3 This is one solution.
4 a, c and e

Fibonacci numbers (page 81)

1 55, 89, 144, 233, 377, 610

2 a 20: one less than the eighth term
   b 33: one less than the ninth term
   c 143: one less than the twelfth term

3 If we consider three consecutive Fibonacci numbers, the square of the middle number is either one more *or* one less than the product of the first and last terms.

4 The product of the first and last of these numbers and the product of the middle two always differ by 1.

5 a $1^2 + 12 + 2^2 + 3^2 + 5^2 = 5 \times 8$
      $1^2 + 1^2 + 2^2 + 3^2 + 5^2 + 8^2 = 8 \times 13$
      $1^2 + 1^2 + 2^2 + 3^2 + 5^2 + 8^2 + 13^2 = 13 \times 21$
      $1^2 + 1^2 + 2^2 + 3^2 + 5^2 + 8^2 + 13^2 + 21^2 = 21 \times 34$
   b $3^3 + 5^3 - 2^3 = 144$
      $5^3 + 8^3 - 3^3 = 610$
      $8^3 + 13^3 - 5^3 = 2584$

6 Some examples for which this is true:
   $1 + 1 + 2 + 3 + 5 + 8 + 13 + 21 + 34 + 55 = 143 = 11 \times 13$
   $1 + 2 + 3 + 5 + 8 + 13 + 21 + 34 + 55 + 89 = 231 = 11 \times 21$

7 a Divisible by 2 (an even number)
   b Divisible by 3 (a multiple of 3)
   c Divisible by 5 (a multiple of 5)
   d Divisible by 8 (a multiple of 8)

Repeating cycles (page 82)

1 a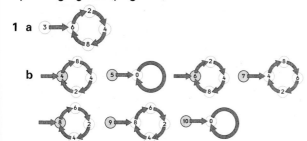

   b

2 a   b 7, 14, 21, 28, 35, 42, 49, 56, 63, 70, 77, 84, 91, 98, 105...

   c → 2 → 4 → 6 → 8 → 0 ↺
      → 3 → 6 → 9 → 2 → 5 → 8 → 1 → 4 → 7 → 0 ↺
      → 5 → 0 ↺
      → 6 → 2 → 8 → 4 → 0 ↺
      → 8 → 6 → 4 → 2 → 0 ↺
      → 9 → 8 → 7 → 6 → 5 → 4 → 3 → 2 → 1 → 0 ↺

Power cycling (page 83)

1 $2^7 = 128, \ 2^8 = 256, \ 2^9 = 512, \ 2^{10} = 1024$.
   The unit digits show that these numbers fit the cycle.

2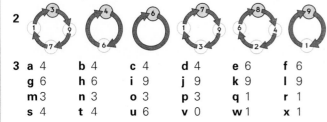

3 a 4   b 4   c 4   d 4   e 6   f 6
   g 6   h 6   i 9   j 9   k 9   l 9
   m 3   n 3   o 3   p 3   q 1   r 1
   s 4   t 4   u 6   v 0   w 1   x 1

In a canoe (page 84)

1 8 moves   2 15 moves   3 24 moves

4 The smallest number of moves is the number of boys (or girls) multiplied by the number two greater than this.
   2 boys × 4 = 8 ⎫ 7
   3 boys × 5 = 15 ⎬ 9
   4 boys × 6 = 24 ⎬ 11
   ∴ 5 boys × 7 = 35 ⎭

Happy numbers (page 85)

1 32 is also happy.

2 Since 13 and 10 also reach 1, they too are happy.

3 HAPPY: 7, 10, 13, 19, 23, 28, 31, 32, 44, 49
   SAD: all other numbers

4 Since 4 is sad, so is 40; since 3 is sad so is 30. Since 42 is sad, so is 24: any 2-digit numbers consisting of identical digits reversed are the same type. Once we enter a cycle that we know will be sad, it is not necessary to continue.

Mixed challenges (page 86)

1 14   2 Jolly 20, Bossy 2, Sporty 11, Popular 28, Helpful 14

3 20   4 K = 2, L = 5, M = 12   5 a 11   b 7

Logic puzzles (page 87)

1 45 min.   2 12 cuts

3 When they meet, they are the same distance from Sydney.

4 a 9:59 a.m.   b 9:58 a.m.

5   6   7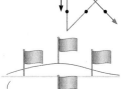

8 Three flags in one horizontal plane form an equilateral triangle, and one flag could be on top of a hill or in a valley.

9

Students may assume that the squares are to be the same size.

10 Divide the coins into three piles of three and compare the first two. If A balances B, then C contains the heavier coin. If A does not balance B, the heavier side contains the heavier coin. Now take the heavier pile and compare two of the three coins. As in weighing the three piles, the heavier coin will be obvious.

Models or diagrams (page 88)

1 20 minutes

2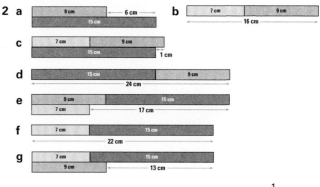

3 9 m   4 a 2 hrs 20 min.   b $4\frac{1}{2}$ hrs

5 a 70 min.   b 110 min.

Perimeter and area

1 The length of a rectangle is four times its width.
If the perimeter is 60 cm, find: the length _____ the width. _____

2 The perimeter of a square is 24 cm. What is the area? _____

3 The area of a square is 64 cm². What is the perimeter? _____

4 The length of a rectangle is 5 cm more than its width.
If the perimeter is 42 cm, what is the length?

_____

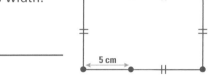

5 The perimeter of a rectangle is 26 cm.
If the length is 3 cm more than the width, what is the area? _____

6 Two sides of a triangle are equal and the third side is half
as long. Find the length of each side if the perimeter of the
triangle is:

a 15 cm _____ **b** 35 cm. _____

7 This figure is formed by 5 squares of the same size.

a If the perimeter of the figure
is 48 cm, what is its area? _____

b If the 5 squares have a total area of 45 cm²,
what is the perimeter of the figure? _____

c If the area of the figure is 32 000 cm²,
find the perimeter of the figure. _____

8 Draw rectangles having the following perimeters and areas.

	Perimeter	Area
a	10 cm	4 cm²
b	10 cm	6 cm²
c	12 cm	5 cm²
d	12 cm	8 cm²

Perimeter challenges

1 A square piece of paper is folded in half, as shown.
If the resulting rectangle has a perimeter of 24 cm,
what was the perimeter of the original square?

_____

2 The square in this diagram has been divided into three
congruent (identical) rectangles. If the perimeter of one of
these rectangles is 16 cm, what is the perimeter of
the square?

_____

3 This 9 m × 9 m square garden has been divided into three
rectangles. If all the rectangles have the same area,
 what are the measurements of each one?

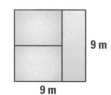

9 m

_____

9 m

4 A square has an area of 36 cm².

a If this square is divided into nine congruent squares,
how many centimetres are there in
the perimeter of one of the nine? _____

b It is now divided into six congruent rectangles.
How many centimetres are there
in the perimeter of one of the six? _____

5 A square has an area of 144 cm².

a If this square is divided into twelve congruent rectangles in two ways, as
shown in **i** and **ii**, what is the perimeter of one of the rectangles in each case?

i   _____   **ii**   _____

b If it is divided into congruent rectangles so that each has a
perimeter of 18 cm, what is the total number of rectangles? _____

Area challenges

1 What is the greatest number of 5 cm × 6 cm rectangular cards that can be cut from a rectangular sheet measuring 50 cm × 66 cm? _____

2 How many tiles are needed to completely cover a wall 3 m × 9 m with tiles measuring 20 cm × 30 cm? _____

3 This figure consists of 6 congruent (identical) squares.

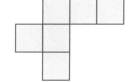

    a If the area is 294 cm², what is the perimeter? _____

    b If the perimeter is 42 cm, what is the area? _____

4 **a** All the shapes in this figure are squares. If the tiny square has an area of 1 cm² and A has an area of 64 cm², what is the area of **H**? _____

        Hint: First find the length of a side of square A, then the length of a side of square B.

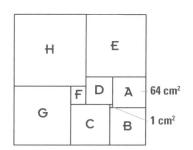

    b Find the area of the other squares.

5 Marcia cut exactly 2 m of ribbon. It went around this box once, leaving 50 cm to tie a big bow. How high was the box? _____

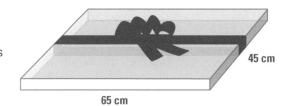

6 Mindy is wrapping a present. She wants to put ribbon around the box in the way illustrated. How much ribbon does she need if she wants to leave 20 cm to tie a bow? _____

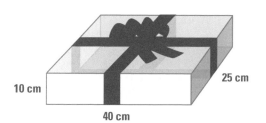

7 Raffy remembers the areas of the faces of these boxes, but not the dimensions. (The dimensions are the length, the width and the height.) Can you help him find the dimensions of the boxes?

a
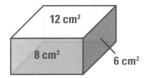

    length _____

    width _____

    height _____

b
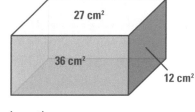

    length _____

    width _____

    height _____

Paving stones

1 A square garden is surrounded by square paving stones.
The garden is the shaded area.

Complete the pattern below to find the relationship between the length of the garden and the number of paving stones needed.

 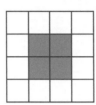 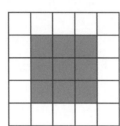 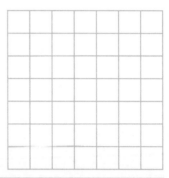

Length of side of garden	1	2	3	4
Number of paving stones	8			

a Draw the fourth pattern and complete the table.

b Work out how to find the number of paving stones needed for a garden with a side length of 10. Try to find your solution in two or three different ways.

_____

c Can you find the rule that describes the relationship?
Can you give a few different rules? _____

_____

d Work out how to find the number of paving
stones needed for a garden with a side length of 30. _____

e Find the length of the side of the garden
if 84 paving stones are needed. _____

2 A garden, 4 m by 5 m, is enclosed by a footpath of width 2 m.

a Find the area of the footpath in square metres. _____

b If the footpath is made up of 1-metre-square
paving stones, how many are used? _____

c If the footpath is extended to a width of 3 metres, adding one more row of
1-metre-square paving stones on the outside,
how many more paving stones are needed? _____

3 A rectangular patio 12 m by 20 m is covered with 1-metre-square tiles.
Black paving stones form the border, and brown paving stones form the interior.
How many paving stones of each colour are there?

_____ black, _____ brown

Area explorations

1 Mrs Jones wants to build a fence around a rectangular vegetable garden using 48 m of new fencing, but keeping part of an existing fence as one side of the garden.

The existing fence is very long and any part of it can be used. The vegetable garden can be any rectangular shape as long as its measurements are in whole numbers. Here are two possibilities.

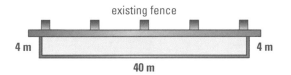

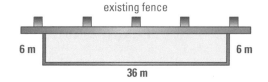

Draw other possible rectangular shapes for the vegetable garden, and find the area of each one.

Working systematically, complete this table to a length of 10 m in your book to find the dimensions of the garden with the largest area.

Length (m)	Breadth (m)	Area (m²)
46	1	46
44	2	
42	3	

2 A large square, C, has an area equal to the sum of the areas of two smaller squares, A and B. Find the length of a side of square C if:

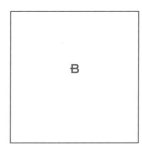

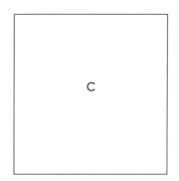

a each side of square A is 3 cm and each side of square B is 4 cm _____

b each side of square A is 5 cm and each side of square B is 12 cm _____

c each side of square A is 6 cm and each side of square B is 8 cm. _____

3 In this diagram the areas of two rectangles are given and all side measurements are whole numbers. The perimeter of the shaded rectangle is 28 cm. If A is a square, what is the area of the shaded rectangle? _____

88 cm²	A
	24 cm²

See Teacher's Book for grid paper.

Cough medicine

A full bottle of cough medicine contains 200 mL.

1 Gary is 8 years old and his mum has just bought
this bottle of cough mixture.
He needs to take some cough mixture every day
between 8 a.m. and 8 p.m., every 4 hours.

    a How many times
will he take it a day? _____

    b How many millilitres
will Gary take a day? _____

    c In a full bottle how many
5 mL doses are there? _____

    d If he continues to take the medicine till the
bottle is finished, for how many
days will a bottle last? _____

Cough Medicine
Dosage
- children over 12 years: 10 mL
- children 6–12 years: 5 mL
- children 2–6 years: 2·5 mL

To be taken every 4 hours

2 Anton is 14 years old. He is very ill and has a new bottle of this cough medicine.
He will take his first dose at 7 a.m. and his last dose at 11 p.m. He will take some
cough mixture every 4 hours.

    a How many times will he take it a day? _____

    b How many millilitres will Anton take a day? _____

    c In a full bottle how many 10 mL doses are there? _____

    d If he continues to take the medicine till the
bottle is finished, for how many days will it last? _____

    e If Anton's first dose of medicine was at 7 a.m. on Saturday,
when will he take the last dose from the bottle? _____

3 Baby Frances is 3 years old. She is very ill and has a new bottle of this cough
medicine. She has to take a dose between 6 a.m. and 10 p.m., every 4 hours.

    a How many times will she take it in a day? _____

    b How many millilitres will Frances take a day? _____

    c In a full bottle how many 2·5 mL doses are there? _____

    d If she continues to take the medicine till the
bottle is finished, for how many days will a bottle last? _____

    e If Frances's first dose of medicine was at 6 a.m. on Saturday,
when will she take the last dose from the bottle? _____

Volume & surface area

Equipment: cubes

1 Cubes can grow! Using 1 cm cubes, build a 2 cm cube, a 3 cm cube and a 4 cm cube.
Now complete the table below for each of these solids, and then continue the pattern.
Each cube has _____ edges and _____ faces.

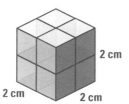

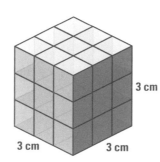

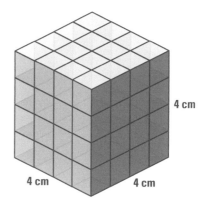

Length of side (cm)	1	2	3	4	5	6
Total edge length (cm)	12					
Surface area (cm²)	6					
Volume (cm³)	1					

2 Find the volume of a cube given that the sum of all the edges is 36 cm. _____

Now find its total surface area. _____

3 The volume of a rectangular prism box is 24 cm³. Complete the table below for each possible prism.

Length	Width	Height	Total surface area
24	1	1	
12	1	2	
8	1	3	
6	2	2	
4	3	2	

4 **a** If the volume of the cubic box in which 8 balls fit exactly is 512 cm³, find the radius of each ball.

_____

Hint: First find the length of the side of the cube.

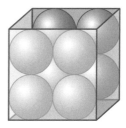

b Find the volume of the cubic box if 8 balls, whose radius is 3 cm each, fit exactly into this box. _____

Volume and capacity

1   How many cube boxes with sides of 3 cm can
    be placed in this cardboard box measuring
    12 cm by 9 cm by 6 cm?

    _____

    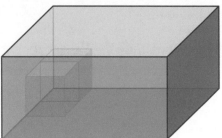

    Hint: First work out how many cube boxes
    are in the bottom layer.

2   How many cubical blocks measuring 2 cm × 2 cm × 2 cm will fit into a case
    measuring:

    a   10 cm × 10 cm × 4 cm?   _____

    b   10 cm × 20 cm × 8 cm?   _____

    c   20 cm × 20 cm × 20 cm?   _____

    d   1 m × 40 cm × 20 cm?   _____

3   Boxes measuring 10 cm by 20 cm by 4 cm are packed in a carton whose
    dimensions are 50 cm by 100 cm by 20 cm.
    What is the maximum number of boxes that can be packed in the carton?

    _____

4   A cube with edges 12 cm long is cut into smaller cubes.

    a   How many small cubes will there be if the smaller cubes have edges of:

    i   6 cm?   _____   **ii**   4 cm?   _____

    b   What is the length of each side of the smaller cubes if there are:

    i   64 cubes?   _____   **ii**   216 cubes?   _____

5   A rectangular block of lead measuring 12 cm by 8 cm by 6 cm is melted and made
    into a block 9 cm long and 4 cm wide. What is the height of the block?

    _____

6   A wooden cube that is 2 cm on each side has a mass of 16 grams.
    What is the mass of a similar wooden cube that is 6 cm on each side?

    _____

Measurement

Volume investigation

For both these exercises, set out your work in a table as shown.
From 1 cm squared paper, cut out four 10 cm squares. Take one of these and cut a 1 cm square from each corner, as shown. Fold along the dotted lines to make an open box.
Now calculate the volume of the box.

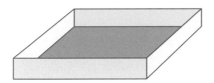

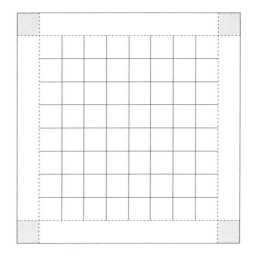

Take another 10 cm square. This time cut a 2 cm square from each corner. Fold, and calculate the volume. From a third square, cut 3 cm squares from the corners and from a fourth, 4 cm squares, folding each and calculating their volume.

Complete the table below for the different squares and calculate the volume of each box after the various squares have been cut from each corner.

Size of paper (cm)	Size of cut square (cm)	Size of box (cm)	Volume of box (cm³)
10 × 10	1 × 1	1 × 8 × 8	
	2 × 2	2 × 6 × 6	
	3 × 3		
	4 × 4		
12 × 12	1 × 1		
	2 × 2		
	3 × 3		
	4 × 4		
	5 × 5		
14 x 14	1 × 1		
	2 × 2		
	3 × 3		
	4 × 4		
	5 × 5		
	6 × 6		
15 x 15	1 × 1		
	2 × 2		
	3 × 3		
	4 × 4		
	5 × 5		
	6 × 6		
	7 × 7		

See *Teacher's Book* for grid paper.

Volume

1 A tin whose base is a rectangle 10 cm by 20 cm contains 1 litre of water. What is the depth of the water? _____

2 A stone of volume 120 cm³ is thrown into this container which is filled 2 cm high with water.

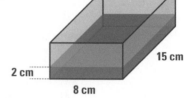

15 cm

2 cm

8 cm

   a What is the new height of the water level?

   _____

   b If the container is 5 cm high, what extra volume of stone can be thrown into the container to fill it completely? _____

3 A rectangular tank of height 12 cm and base 5 cm by 7 cm is filled with water to a height of 8 cm.

   a By how much will the water level rise if a stone of volume 70 cm³ is dropped into the tank? _____

   b What volume of stone could have been dropped into this tank to fill it completely? _____

4 A rectangular container with base measurements 6 cm × 5 cm has fluid in it to a height of 8 cm. If this fluid is now poured into a container with a square base, 4 cm × 4 cm, what height will the fluid reach?

_____

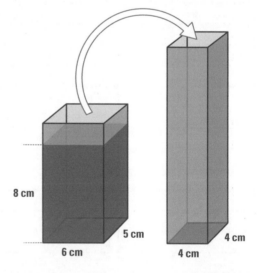

8 cm

5 cm

6 cm

4 cm

4 cm

5 A square-based prism of height 8 cm is dropped into this cylinder containing 800 mL of water. The water and the prism now have a volume of 1 L.

   a Find the volume of the prism. _____

   b Find the length of the square base. _____

Scale drawings

1 **a** The scale drawing of a rectangular room measures 10 cm by 6 cm.

    i If the actual length of the room is 30 m,
what is the actual perimeter of the room in metres? _____

    ii If the actual width of the room is 9 m,
what is the actual perimeter of the room in metres? _____

	Length	Width
Scale	10 cm	6 cm
Actual	30 m	
Actual		9 m

b The scale drawing of a rectangular room measures 12 cm by 8 cm.

    i If the actual width of the room is 12 m,
what is the actual perimeter of the room in metres? _____

    ii If the actual length of the room is 30 m,
what is the actual perimeter of the room in metres? _____

	Length	Width
Scale	12 cm	8 cm
Actual		12 m
Actual	30 m	

2 A building plan uses a scale of 1 cm to represent 3 m.

    a What distances are represented by the following lengths on the plan:

        i 5 cm _____   **ii** 1 mm _____   **iii** 1.5 cm? _____

    b What distances are drawn on the plan if the actual building has these measurements:

        i 33 m _____   **ii** 3.6 m _____   **iii** 150 m? _____

3 On a certain map, 1 cm represents 20 km. If two towns are
really 140 km apart, how far apart are they on the map? _____

4 On another map, a distance of 250 km was represented by a 5 cm line. Work out
the distance represented by lines of:

    a 3 cm _____   **b** 7 cm. _____

5 A railway engine is 15 m long. To build a model railway to $\frac{1}{100}$ scale,
what will the length of the model engine be in centimetres? _____

Ratio problems

1 A floor-tiler uses 4 grey tiles to every 3 yellow ones.

    a If he wants to use 80 grey tiles, how many yellow tiles does he need? _____

    b If he uses 150 yellow tiles, how many grey tiles will there be? _____

    c If he uses 420 tiles *altogether*, how many grey ones will he need? _____

2 When Julian went shopping, he found that 2 cricket balls cost the same amount as 3 tennis balls. He bought 9 tennis balls for $12.

    a How many cricket balls could he have bought for this amount? _____

    b How much would 15 tennis balls cost? _____

    c How many tennis balls would he get for $32? _____

    d How many cricket balls would he get for $32? _____

3 A concrete mixture was made up of 4 parts of metal to 3 parts of sand to 1 part of cement. Find the quantity of each material needed to make:

    a 16 cubic metres of concrete; _____

    b 40 cubic metres of concrete. _____

4 At a certain time, a tree 6 m high casts a 4 m shadow.

    a At the same time, the shadow of a nearby building is 12 m long. How high is the building? _____

    b How long is the shadow of a 12 m pole at that time? _____

    c How long is the shadow of a 21 m building at that time? _____

5 At another time, the 6 metre-high pole casts a 2·5 m shadow. At this time:

    a a building casts a 10 m shadow. Find the height of the building. _____

    b a pole's shadow is 3·75 m. How high is this pole? _____

6 A car uses 6 L of petrol to travel 72 km.

    a Calculate the distance it would travel if the petrol tank contained:

        i 54 L _____   **ii** 2 L _____   **iii** 8 L. _____

    b Calculate the number of litres of petrol used when the car travels:

        i 36 km _____   **ii** 24 km _____   **iii** 108 km. _____

Ratio and proportion

1 Divide $24 between two people so that one has:

   a twice as much as the other; _____ and _____

   b three times as much as the other; _____ and _____

   c five times as much as the other. _____ and _____

2 Divide $60 between two people so that one has:

   a twice as much as the other; _____ and _____

   b three times as much as the other; _____ and _____

   c four times as much as the other. _____ and _____

3 A concrete mixture was made up of 4 parts of metal to 3 parts of sand to 2 parts of cement. Find the quantity of each material needed to make 27 cubic metres of concrete.

Metal	Sand	Cement	Concrete
4	3	2	
			27 cubic metres

4 A soccer team in one season won four times as many matches as they lost. If they played 15 matches in this season, how many matches did they win? _____

5 Divide $28 between Kumiko, Masika and Inika in such a way that Masika gets twice as much as Kumiko, and Inika gets twice as much as Masika. _____

6 Gilah, Jahinger and Olga buy a $10 lottery ticket. Gilah pays $5, Jahinger $3 and Olga $2. If the ticket wins a $2000 prize and the prize is shared in the same ratio as the contributions to the ticket, how much should each person receive? _____

7 Mr and Mrs Kind decide to share $240 equally between their children for the summer vacation. When the eldest got a holiday job, he divided his share equally between all his brothers and sisters.

If each child was given an extra $8, how many children are there in the Kind family? _____

8 A dog is chasing a rat. They are 9 metres apart. For every 7 metres that the dog runs, the rat runs 4 metres. How far does the dog have to run in order to catch the rat? _____

Measurement

Rate problems

1 Twenty-four boarders in a school eat 20 kg of potatoes a week. At this rate, how many kilograms are needed for this period for 18 boarders? _____

2 A factory produces 344 tables in 8 hours. If the production rate is always the same:

    a how many tables would it produce in 1 hour? _____

    b how many tables would it produce in 3 hours? _____

    c how long would it take to produce 430 tables? _____

3 Clayton can cut a log into five pieces in 20 minutes. At the same rate, how long would it take to cut the log into six pieces? _____

4 Dmitri has worked for 3 hours while Lindsay has worked for 4 hours at a job. If they are paid at the same rate and together they received $84, how much did each man get?

    Dimitri _____   Lindsay _____

5 If 4 cans of food will feed 3 dogs for 1 day:

    a how many cans are needed to feed 6 dogs for 5 days? _____

    b for how long will 48 cans feed 6 dogs? _____

6 At a drink-bottling factory, each tap fills 5 bottles every 20 seconds. If there are 20 taps operating and each tap is filling the bottles at the same rate, how many bottles should be filled each minute? _____

7 In a certain country, telephone rates are 25c for the first minute and 11c for each additional minute.

    a How much would it cost to make a 5 minute call? _____

    b If a telephone call cost $1.13, how long did it last? _____

8 A car-rental company charges $45 a day and 12c for each kilometre for a five-seater car.

    a If the Liu family rented a car for 5 days and drove 800 km, what was the total cost of rental? _____

    b If Mr Campbell rented a car for 2 days and paid $132, how many kilometres did he drive? _____

9 A small car uses 30 litres to travel 450 km.

    a At this rate, what is the maximum distance the car can travel on 20 litres of petrol? _____

    b How far can the car travel on 1 litre of petrol? _____

    c Find the number of litres used to travel 600 km. _____

    d Petrol costs $1.20 per litre. Find the cost of the petrol to travel 150 km. _____

    e If the tank holds 75 litres, at this rate, how far can it travel on a full tank? _____

Measurement

Dripping tap

1 The tap is dripping at a rate of 2 drops every second. Five drops of water make 1 mL.

    a How many drops in 1 minute? _____

    b How much water drips in 1 minute? _____

2 Luke placed a dish under a dripping tap to save wasting water. The tap is dripping at a rate of 10 drops every minute. Five drops of water make 4 mL.

    a How many millilitres will be collected each minute? _____

    b How many millilitres will be collected after 1 hour? _____

    c How many litres will be collected after 10 hours? _____

    d How long will it take to collect 80 mL? _____

    e How long will it take to collect 200 mL? _____

    f How long will it take to collect 5 litres? _____

3 A tap drips 20 drops every minute. William placed a bottle under the tap and collected 240 mL of water in 1 hour.

    a How many millilitres were collected in 1 minute? _____

    b How many drops in 1 hour? _____

    c How many of these drops make 1 mL? _____

    d What is the volume of each drip? _____

    e How many litres per day can William collect? _____

4 A faulty tap is dripping at a rate of 5 drops every minute. Six drops of water make 1 cm^3. An old ice-cream container with a square base of 10 cm is placed under the dripping tap to save the dripping water.

    a Find the volume of water that drips in 1 hour. _____

    b Find how long it will take for the water to reach a height of 5 cm.

    _____

Speed challenges

1 A car travels at 90 km/h. Assuming that it travels at constant speed, calculate the following:

   a speed in metres per hour; _____

   b speed in metres per minute; _____

   c speed in metres per second; _____

   d time taken to travel 360 km; _____

   e time taken to travel 120 km; _____

   f distance travelled in $1\frac{1}{2}$ hours; _____

   g distance travelled in 10 minutes; _____

   h number of metres travelled in 1 minute. _____

2 **a** If a car travels at 72 km/h, how far does it travel in one second? Express your answer in metres. _____

   b If a car travels at 15 m/sec, how far does it travel in one hour? Express your answer in kilometres. _____

3 A train running between two stations 50 km apart arrives on time if it averages 60 km/h. How late will it be if it averages 50 km/h? _____

4 Gabriella cycled for 3 hours and travelled 48 km.
Then she cycled for 2 hours and travelled 27 km.

What was her average speed
for the whole journey? _____

(Note that average speed $= \dfrac{\text{total distance}}{\text{total time}}$)

5 Adam drives for 80 km at an average speed of 60 km/h and then he drives for 30 km at 45 km/h. What was Adam's average speed for the entire trip? _____

6 A motorist travelled at an average speed of 48 km/h for $1\frac{1}{3}$ hours and then drove another 56 km in $\frac{2}{3}$ of an hour. What was her average speed for the whole journey?

_____

7 Angelica starts on a walk at 5 kilometres an hour. Three hours later, on the same route, Janelle starts riding her bicycle at 11 kilometres an hour. When will Janelle overtake Angelica? _____

Speed problems

1 Malcolm set out to walk a distance of 12 kilometres. After walking for $1\frac{1}{2}$ hours at a steady speed of $5\frac{1}{2}$ km/h, he had to slow down to a steady pace of 3 km/h which he maintained till the end of the journey.

How long did he take to complete the journey? _____

2 When Nicole and her brother Ivan walk to school, Nicole walks at an average of 80 steps per minute while Ivan walks at an average of 90 steps per minute. Each of Nicole's steps are 81 cm long and she takes 12 minutes to walk to school.

   a If each of Ivan's steps are 72 cm long,
      how long does Ivan take to walk to school? _____

   b If Ivan took 16 minutes to walk to school,
      how long are each of his steps then? _____

3 **a** David drives at an average speed of 60 km/h, while Michelle drives at an average speed of 75 km/h. If they both drive 25 km, which person completes the trip first, and by how many minutes?

      _____

   b Jason drives at an average speed of 45 km/h, while Paul drives at an average speed of 40 km/h. If they both have to drive 15 km to the airport, how long does Jason have to wait for Paul to arrive? _____

4 The graph below represents the journey of a cyclist from home and back. As you can see, after 1 hour the cyclist was 15 km from home.

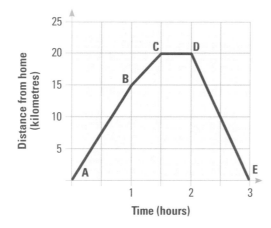

   a When is the cyclist not cycling? _____

   b When is the cyclist travelling fastest? _____

   c How far did the cyclist travel altogether? _____

   d What is the average speed for the whole trip? _____

   e How much faster is she travelling in the
      leg D to E compared with the leg A to B? _____

Cutting rectangles

Equipment: scissors

Use 1 cm squared paper to solve problems 1, 2, 3 and 5. Copy the figures, cut them out and experiment.

1 If a 6 cm × 3 cm rectangular piece of wood is cut as shown and the two pieces are put together to form a longer but narrower rectangle, what are the dimensions of the new rectangle?

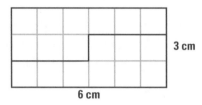

_____

2 How can you cut a rectangular piece of wood measuring 8 cm × 3 cm to make a rectangle that measures 12 cm × 2 cm?

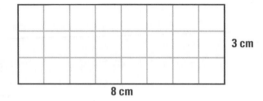

3 What are the two ways in which you can cut an 8 cm × 6 cm rectangular piece of wood to form a 12 cm × 4 cm rectangle, using only one cut in each case?

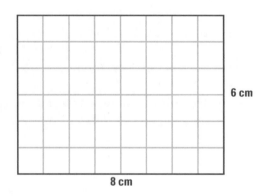

4 Show how you would cut this 9 cm × 4 cm rectangle to change it into a 6 cm × 6 cm square.

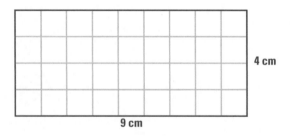

5 We can change a 25 × 16 rectangle into a 20 × 20 square by cutting equal steps, as illustrated.

Use 0.5 cm squared paper to show how this can be done.

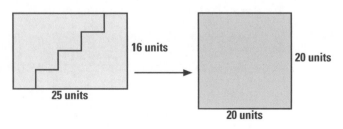

See *Teacher's Book* for grid paper.

Solids

Equipment: cubes

1 Build each of the figures below, then draw the view you would get of each one from the top, from the front and from the left side.

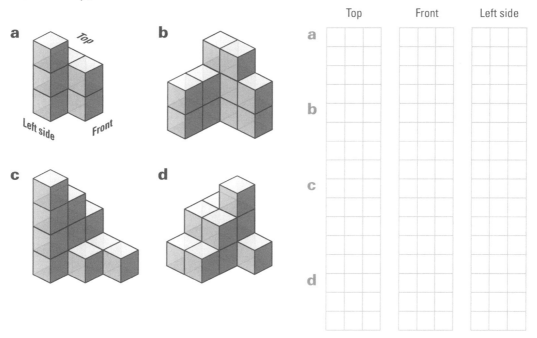

a

b

c

d

Top   Front   Left side

a

b

c

d

2 Use cubes to build the figures that from the top, the front and the left side would show you the following shapes. Draw your solid on the isometric grid on the right.

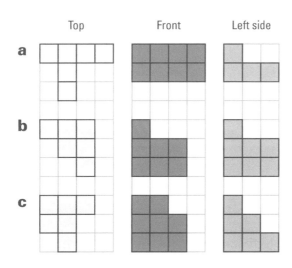

Top   Front   Left side

a

b

c

Nets

Equipment: scissors

Nets are drawn figures that can be folded to form solid shapes.

1 Name the solids for these nets.

a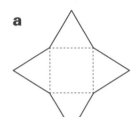

b

_____

c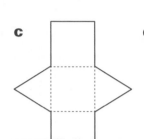

_____

d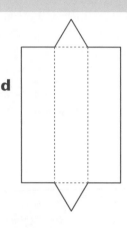

_____

_____

Space

2 Shown below are two nets of a cube. On squared paper, draw as many other different cube nets as you can. Now check all your drawings by cutting them out and folding them into cubes.

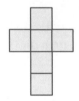 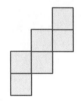

3 On squared paper, draw a net for this rectangular prism. Cut out the drawing and fold it to make sure it forms the correct shape.

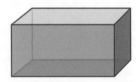

4 Which of these nets can be folded into the square pyramid?

a ⬭ **b** ⬭ **c** ⬭ **d** ⬭ **e** ⬭

   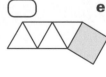 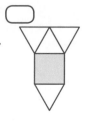

Polygons

The sum of the angles of any triangle is 180°. It is easy to show this by doing the following experiment:

Draw a triangle of any size and mark the angles as shown in **a**.

Cut out the triangle and tear it into three pieces, each containing an angle.

Place the angles next to each other, as shown in **b**. This will produce a straight line, showing that the three angles total 180°.

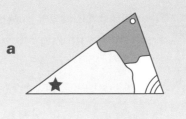

1 Using the fact that you have just proved, find the sum of the angles of these polygons.

| quadrilateral | pentagon | hexagon | heptagon | octagon |

Hint: You may need to draw one or more diagonals, as in the first two figures, to make triangles.

Now complete this table. Note that by 'angle sum' we mean the sum of the interior angles at the vertices (corners) of the polygon.

Sides of polygon	4	5	6	7	8
Number of triangles					
Angle sum (degrees)					

2 What pattern have you found for the angle sum?

_____

3 What is the angle sum for:

a a decagon (a polygon that has 10 sides)? _____

b a dodecagon (a polygon that has 12 sides)? _____

What's my shape?

1 Read these clues very carefully.

From the information they give, name and draw the shape (or shapes) that each one describes.

a I have four equal sides.

b I am a triangle with two sides equal.

c I am a quadrilateral with four right angles (90° angles).

d I am a quadrilateral with both pairs of opposite sides equal.

e I am a quadrilateral with equal diagonals.

f I am a quadrilateral with four equal sides *and* equal diagonals.

g All my points are the same distance from one fixed point.

h I am a triangle with one axis of symmetry.

i I am a triangle with three axes of symmetry.

j I am a quadrilateral with:

    i four axes of symmetry;

    ii two axes of symmetry;

    iii one axis of symmetry.

2 Name these geometric solids and draw each one.

a I have 6 square faces. _____

b I have 8 vertices, 12 edges and 6 rectangular faces.
My opposite faces are the same shape (congruent). _____

c I have 4 congruent triangles as my faces. _____

d I have 2 triangular faces and 3 rectangular faces. _____

e I am a solid with no edges or vertices. _____

f I have a square base and 4 congruent, triangular faces. _____

g I am a solid with two circular edges.
My net consists of 2 circles and 1 rectangle. _____

h I have a circular base, 1 vertex, 1 circular edge and 2 faces. _____

i I am a solid with 5 faces, 8 edges and 5 vertices. _____

j I am a solid with 6 faces, 10 edges and 6 vertices. _____

Billiards

A standard billiard table is rectangular in shape and about twice as long as it is wide, but you will be concerned with tables of rather unusual dimensions and with pockets only at the corners.

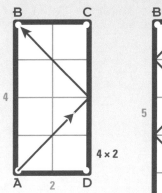 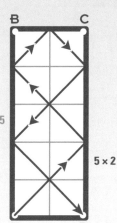 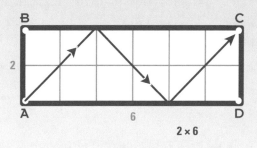

If a ball is hit from corner A at an angle of 45° to the edge of the table, all its rebounds will be at 45°. Eventually it will reach a second corner, and stop. The challenge in these exercises is to draw the path of the ball on tables of different sizes and to determine into which corner pocket it will fall. It always starts in the lower left-hand corner and travels at an angle of 45°.

1 The tables shown above are 4 x 2, 5 x 2 and 2 x 6. Draw a diagram to illustrate each table-size given below, labelling all the tables you draw.

a 1 × 3	**b** 5 × 1	**c** 5 × 3	**d** 7 × 3	**e** 7 × 5
f 2 × 5	**g** 6 × 1	**h** 4 × 3	**i** 2 × 3	**j** 6 × 5
k 7 × 2	**l** 5 × 8	**m** 3 × 4	**n** 7 × 6	**o** 5 × 12
p 2 × 4	**q** 4 × 4	**r** 6 × 6	**s** 6 × 2	**t** 12 × 8

Draw the path of each ball.

2 Look carefully at all your drawings. By making a generalisation, predict into which pocket the ball will fall if the table is:

a odd by odd (e.g. 3 × 1 or 7 × 9) _____ **b** even by odd (e.g. 4 × 3) _____

c odd by even (e.g. 3 × 4) _____ **d** even by even. _____

Consider the 'reduced' table in each case: the 'reduced' size corresponding to a 4 × 4 table will be 1 × 1 and to a 12 × 8 table will be 3 × 2.

Refer to corner A as lower left, corner B as upper left, corner C as upper right and corner D as lower right.

3 Investigate the number of times the ball hits the sides of a table before it falls into a corner; again you will have to consider the 'reduced' dimensions for each table. Note that the first and the final corner positions do not count as 'hits'.

See *Teacher's Book* for grid paper.

Cube explorations

1 Examine the solid on the right.

    a How many small cubes
are needed to build it? _____

    b How many small cubes can
you actually see in this view? _____

    c How many small cubes
cannot be seen in this view? _____

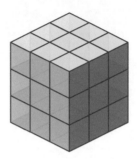

2 Now look at the second large cube.

    a How many small cubes
are needed to build it? _____

    b How many small cubes
can you see in this view? _____

    c How many small cubes
are hidden in this view? _____

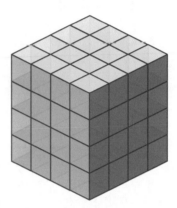

3 A block of cheese is covered with wax and then cut into 1 cm cubes. Given the
measurements of the cheese, complete this table to show in each case.

    • how many cubes can be cut,

    • how many cubes will have wax on them and

    • how many will not have wax on them.

Size of cheese	Cubes cut	Cubes with wax	Cubes without wax
3 cm × 3 cm × 3 cm			
4 cm × 4 cm × 4 cm			
5 cm × 5 cm × 5 cm			
6 cm × 6 cm × 6 cm			
10 cm × 10 cm × 10 cm			
8 cm × 6 cm × 4 cm			
7 cm × 5 cm × 4 cm			

Experiments with cubes

Equipment: cubes (centicubes)

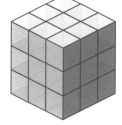

1 Some small cubes have been stacked and glued together to form a larger cube. Use centicubes to build this 3 × 3 × 3 cube, and answer the following questions.

    a How many small cubes are in the large cube? _____

    b If this large cube is dropped into a bucket of red paint and completely submerged so that it is red on all the outside faces:

        i how many small cubes have three red faces? _____

        ii how many small cubes have two red faces? _____

        iii how many small cubes have one red face only? _____

        iv how many small cubes have no red paint on any face? _____

    c Find the sum of your answers to **b i–iv** and compare it with your answer to **a**. _____

2 This time a 4 × 4 × 4 cube is built.

Can you answer all parts of exercise **1** with reference to the larger cube?

    a _____

    b i _____   **ii** _____

       iii _____   **iv** _____

3 Can you make a comment about any of your results?

_____

4 I have one small red cube and I want to enclose it with small blue cubes to make one large blue cube.

    a How many blue cubes do I need to do this? _____

    b How many small yellow cubes will I need if I want to enclose the blue cube and make an even larger yellow one? _____

5 Repeat questions **a** and **b** in exercise **4**, starting with eight small red cubes instead of one—that is, with a red cube measuring 2 × 2 × 2.

    a _____   **b** _____

Curves from lines

1 Can you draw a circle using only a ruler and a pencil?
To do this:

- Mark a dot on the page.
- Place your ruler so that the dot is just visible on one side of it; then, holding the ruler firmly, draw a line on the other side of it.
- Move the ruler slightly and again follow the previous instruction. Do this many, many times.
- Continue to move the ruler slightly until it has turned in a complete circle around the dot.

2 Can you draw a parabola using a ruler and a pencil only?

a Draw two intersecting equal lines. On each one, mark and number points the same distance apart, with the numbers running in opposite directions. With your ruler, join 1 to 1, 2 to 2, and so on, on all corresponding numbers.

The resulting curve is called a parabola.

The closer the points and the more you have, the smoother will be your curve.

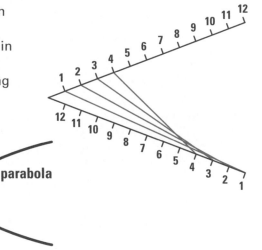

b On squared paper, draw a square with sides of 11 cm and number the points as shown. Use the above methods and coloured pencils to construct four intersecting parabolas.

c Construct parabolas by marking and joining corresponding points on enlarged versions of these shapes.

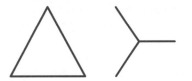

d Make up some of your own designs, using coloured pencils or pens.

See *Teacher's Book* for grid paper.

More curves

1 The 36 points on the circumference of this circle carry the numbers 1 to 72 in a double row so that each point has two numbers, the inner line numbering 1 to 36 and the outer 37 to 72.

With coloured pencils (or pens), create different circle patterns by drawing a straight line:

   a between each number and the number that is 8 units more—for example, join 1 to 9, 2 to 10, 3 to 11, 4 to 12 and so on till 64 to 72.

   b between each number and the number that is 12 more, and then the one that is 16 more.

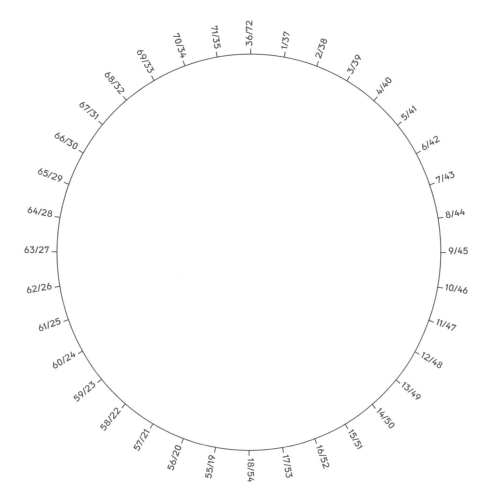

2 Using other copies of this circle, join each number to the number that is twice (double) itself, so that you join 1 to 2, 2 to 4, 3 to 6 and so on. The resulting shape is called a *cardioid*.

3 Think of other rules to join numbers. What patterns can you make?

Euler's formula

A Swiss mathematician called Leonard Euler (1707–83) discovered a relationship between the number of faces, the number of vertices and the number of edges of a solid.

- The flat surface of a solid is called a *face*.
- Two faces meet on an *edge*.
- Edges meet at a *vertex* (plural: vertices).

So the mathematical name for corners is *vertices*.

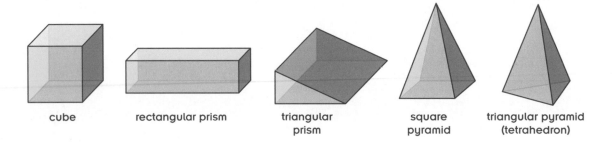

cube   rectangular prism   triangular prism   square pyramid   triangular pyramid (tetrahedron)

1 Complete this table with reference to the solids above.

Solid	Number of faces (F)	Number of vertices (V)	Number of edges (E)	F + V − E
Cube				
Rectangular prism				
Triangular prism				
Square pyramid				
Triangular pyramid				

2 Can you find Euler's formula? If you can, test your solution on the figures below.

a

b

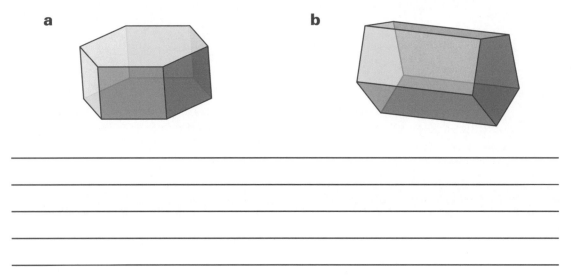

_____

_____

_____

_____

_____

LOCUS

Equipment: string and pencil

Draw and shade the greatest shape (the maximum area) that a goat can graze if he is tied with 5 m long rope and the rope is attached as in the following diagrams. (You should experiment by tying a 5 cm long string to a pencil and tracing the path of the pencil.)

1 To a stake:

2 To a straight 6 m fence (the rope can slide along both sides of the fence):

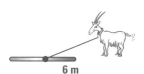

3 To a circular fence (the rope can slide along the outside of the fence):

4 To the corner of a shed that measures 8 m × 10 m:

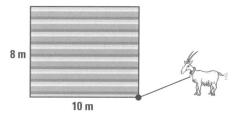

5 To a stake inside a fenced-off paddock:

a

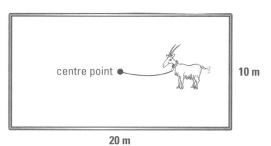

b

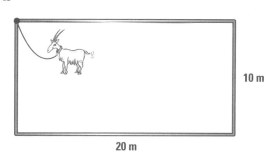

c

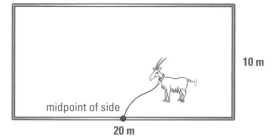

d

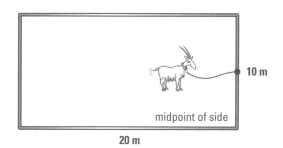

What's my message?

In these messages, letters have replaced numbers. Can you work out my message by finding the values of the letters? Note that in the problems O is the letter O, but in the code for exercise 2 it is the number zero (0).

1

$$\underline{}\;\underline{}\qquad\underline{}\;\underline{}\;\underline{}\qquad\underline{}\;\underline{}\;\underline{}\;\underline{}\;\underline{}\qquad\underline{}\;\underline{}\;\underline{}\;\underline{}\;\underline{}$$

5 3	9 1 7	8 2 4 1 9	9 1 2 6 4

$H \times E = E$

$O^2 = T$

$I^2 = G$

$O + O + O = T$

$T^2 = RH$

$HG \div I = E$

$D \times D = ID$

```
  T H I N           H I T
+ D I R T         -   G O
---------         -------
H G G H D           R N
```

2

$$\underline{}\qquad\underline{}\;\underline{}\;\underline{}\;\underline{}\qquad\underline{}\;\underline{}\;\underline{}\;\underline{}\;\underline{}\;\underline{}\;\underline{}$$

5	8 9 4 6	7 1 3 2 5 3 0

$D - D = G$

$N \times A = N$

$N \times C = E$

$E^2 = NE$

$VG \div V = AG$

$\sqrt{V} = C$

$A + C = N$

$AG - A = O$

```
  D O G         L A N D        C I
+ D O G       - D E A L      + C I
-------       --------       -----
A I L G         I A O         I G
```

Working Mathematically

Simpler problems first

1 Twelve couples, who live in the Happy Retirement Villa, decide to install intercom systems between each of their 12 suites. How many connecting lines are necessary to permit direct conversation between any two suites?

Hint: First solve a simpler problem by considering how many connections are necessary for:

a 2 couples _____

b 3 couples _____

c 4 couples _____

d 5 couples. _____

e Draw up a table and look for a pattern for 12 couples.

2 Some people attended a meeting. If each person shook hands with every other person:

a how many handshakes were there altogether if there were 14 people at the meeting? _____

b how many people attended the meeting if there were 45 handshakes altogether? _____

3 Six students compete in a knockout tennis tournament. The winners of the first match go into the second round and the losers drop out; there are no draws.

After each match the losers drop out, and this process is continued until there is one final winner.

A possible sequence of the tournament, in which five matches were played, is illustrated in this diagram:

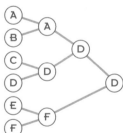

If one more student joined the competition, a possible tournament sequence in which the seven students played six matches could be drawn like this:

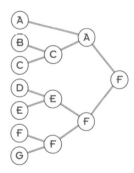

a Draw diagrams illustrating tournaments in which eight and nine students compete. Enter your results in this table:

Number of students	6	7	8	9	20	50
Matches needed to find a winner	5	6				

b Can you predict how many matches must be played in a tournament that includes:

i 20 students? _____

ii 50 students? _____

Now complete the above table.

Logic using scales

In each of these problems the first two sets of scales are balanced. Find the number of ★s needed to balance the third set.

1 If

2 If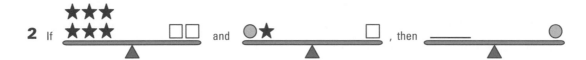

3 If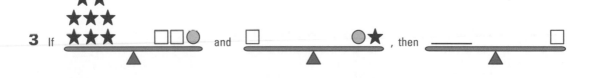

4 If

5 If

6 If

7 If

8 If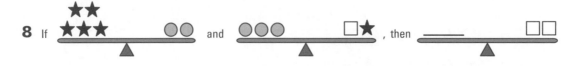

9 If

10 If

Challenge on averages

The average of a set of numbers is found adding the numbers and dividing by how many numbers we added.

For example, to find the average of 3, 7, 11 and 15, since there are 4 numbers, we add these and divide by 4.

$$\therefore \text{average} = \frac{3 + 7 + 11 + 15}{4}$$
$$= \frac{36}{4}$$
$$= 9$$

1   Find the average of:

   a   the first five consecutive numbers;   _____

   b   the first seven consecutive numbers;   _____

   c   the first nine consecutive numbers;   _____

   d   the first three even consecutive numbers (2, 4, 6);   _____

   e   the first nine even consecutive numbers;   _____

   f   the first fifteen consecutive numbers (try to predict).   _____

2   The average mass of three friends is 36 kg. If their masses are three consecutive numbers, what is the mass of the lightest person?   _____

3   The average temperature for five days, Monday to Friday, is 8°C. What is the average temperature from Monday to Wednesday, if the temperatures on the five days are consecutive numbers?   _____

4   The average mass of five cases of fruit is 13 kg. The sixth case of fruit has a mass of 7 kg. What is the average mass of the six cases of fruit?   _____

5   The average age of a group of five children is 12 years. A 24-year-old teacher joins them. What is the average age of all six?   _____

6   The average temperature for five consecutive days is 6°C. If the temperature is 8°C, 5°C, 4°C and 3°C on the first four days, what is the temperature on the fifth day?   _____

7   In three maths tests Jeremy got 72, 78 and 80. What mark will he need in the next maths test in order to have an average score of 80 for all four?   _____

8   The average mass of the eight members of a rowing crew is 72 kg. When the cox joins them, the average mass of crew and cox is 70 kg. Find the mass of the cox.

_____

Working together

1 Fifteen painters can paint a school in 12 days. If 5 extra painters join them just before they start, how long will all 20 painters now take to paint this school?

_____

It can be assumed that all painters work at the same rate.

2 John can paint a room in 3 hours. His apprentice, working alone, requires 6 hours to do the same job.

How long would it take John and his apprentice, working together, to paint the room if they continue to work at the given rates?

Here is a guide to solving the problem.

John can paint 1 room in 3 hours.

John can paint _____ in 1 hour.
His apprentice can paint 1 room in 6 hours.

His apprentice can paint _____ in 1 hour.
Working together, in 1 hour John and his apprentice can paint

_____ + _____ = _____

∴ Together they can paint 1 room in _____ hours.

3 Working alone, Michael can clean the house in 3 hours, while his mother can do the same job in 2 hours.

How long would it take Michael and his mother
to clean the house together if both work at the given rates? _____

4 Lachlan needs 1 hour to do a certain job. His dad can do the same job in $\frac{1}{2}$ hour.
How many minutes will it take them to do
the job if they work together at the given rates? _____

5 Eddie needs 4 days to mow the lawn at the council park. Mark and David, working together, need 3 days to do the same job.

How long will it take Eddie, Mark and David to
do this job if they work together at the given rates? _____

Counting frame mathematics

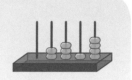

A counting frame uses place values to indicate numbers.

1 Starting from the right, the four beads on the first wire represent 4 ones. The one bead on the next wire represents 1 ten, the three beads on the third wire represent 3 hundreds, while the two beads on the fourth wire represent 2 thousands. Therefore, the number 2314 is represented.

a What numbers are represented on these counting frames?

i 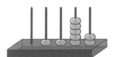 **ii** 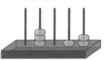 **iii**

_____ _____ _____

b Represent the following numbers on a counting frame.
i 315   **ii** 2031   **iii** 31005

2 On a Martian counting frame, the two beads on the first wire are 2 ones; on the second wire, one bead represents 1 lot of 3; on the third wire, two beads represent 2 lots of 9 ($9 = 3 \times 3$); on the fourth wire, one bead is 1 lot of 27 ($27 = 3 \times 3 \times 3$). The number shown $= 1 \times 27 + 2 \times 9 + 1 \times 3 + 2 = 50$.

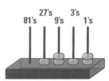

a What numbers would a Martian see on these counting frames?

i  **ii**  **iii**

_____ _____ _____

Note that no wire has more than two beads on it.

b Represent these numbers on a Martian counting frame.
i 4   **ii** 6   **iii** 8   **iv** 12   **v** 15
vi 16   **vii** 30   **viii** 32   **ix** 40   **x** 162

3 In Computerland, the first wire represents ones, the second has lots of 2, the third has lots of 4 (2×2), the fourth has lots of 8 ($2 \times 2 \times 2$), the fifth has lots of 16 ($2 \times 2 \times 2 \times 2$).

a What numbers are represented on these counting frames?

i  **ii**

_____ _____

b Represent the following numbers on a Computerland counting frame.
i 5   **ii** 11   **iii** 14   **iv** 27

Triangular numbers

1 Triangular numbers can be generated by counting the number of spots required to form a triangle.

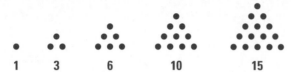

1   **3**   **6**   **10**   **15**

Continuing the above pattern draw the next two shapes.

We can build some interesting patterns and sequences with the triangular numbers.

2

Notice the differences between consecutive triangular numbers, and continue this pattern for the next five terms.

3 Continue this pattern for three more lines.

$$1 = 1$$
$$1 + 2 = 3$$
$$1 + 2 + 3 = 6$$
$$1 + 2 + 3 + 4 = 10$$
$$1 + 2 + 3 + 4 + 5 = 15$$

_____

_____

_____

4 Continue this pattern for three more lines and express it in words. Illustrate (justify) it with diagrams using dots, like this: $1 + 3 = 2^2$

$1 + 3 = 2^2$
$3 + 6 = 3^2$
$6 + 10 = 4^2$
$10 + 15 = 5^2$

5 Continue this pattern for two more lines.

$3 \times 3 - 1 = 8 = 8 \times 1$
$5 \times 5 - 1 = 24 = 8 \times 3$
$7 \times 7 - 1 = 48 = 8 \times 6$
$9 \times 9 - 1 = 80 = 8 \times 10$

_____

_____

6 We can also build the odd squares. Complete the unfinished lines and continue the pattern for two more lines.

$8 \times 1 + 1 = 3^2$
$8 \times 3 + 1 = 5^2$
$8 \times 6 + 1 = 7^2$
$8 \times 10 + 1 =$ _____
$8 \times 15 + 1 =$ _____

_____

_____

7 It can be shown that every positive whole number is either a triangular number or the sum of two or three triangular numbers: 17 = 10 + 6 + 1 or 17 = 15 + 1 + 1.

Show that this is true for the following numbers: 19, 21, 29, 35, 36, 37, 38, 46.

Working Mathematically

Pascal's triangle

This triangular pattern is named after a seventeenth-century French mathematician, Blaise Pascal.

Row		Sum of numbers
	1	
1	1 1	2
2	1 2 1	4
3	1 3 3 1	8
4	1 4 6 4 1	…
5	1 5 10 10 5 1	…

1 Copy these five rows of Pascal's triangle, find the pattern it follows and continue it for the next four rows.

2 Use your calculator to find the value of 11^2, 11^3 and 11^4.
Can you find your answers in the triangle? _____, _____, _____

3 a What is the second number in the sixth row? _____

b What is the second number in the ninth row? _____

c What do you think will be the second number in the fifteenth row? _____

4 a What is the third number in the third row? _____

b What is the third number in the fourth row? _____

c What is the third number in the fifth row? _____

d What pattern do the third numbers form in each row? _____

e What is the third number in the tenth row? _____

5 What is the sum of:

a the first and second numbers in each row? _____

b the second and third numbers in each row? _____

6 What pattern is formed by the third-last numbers in each row? _____

7 a What is the sum of numbers in each of the
first, second, third, fourth, fifth and sixth rows? _____

b What pattern do the sums form? _____

8 Which rows of the triangles will contain only odd numbers? _____

9 What further observations can you make? _____

_____

How many routes?

1 One downward path from P to Q is shown in this figure.

   a How many others can you find?

 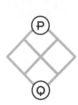  

   b To work out how many routes there are from P to Q on a more complicated figure, it is best to count the number of paths to each intersection. The numbers marking intersections on the figure at right show how many different paths can be taken to reach them.

       Work out and add to the figure the number of different paths there are to each unmarked point.

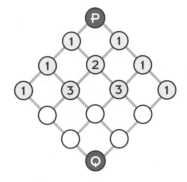

   c By marking the number of possible downwards paths to each intersection in this figure, work out the total number of different paths from P to Q. What do you notice?

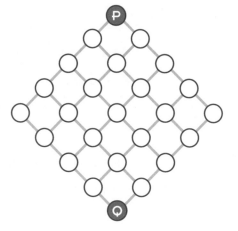

_____

_____

_____

2 Look at these rectangular diagrams. If you travel only on the paths shown and only in the direction of the arrows, how many different routes can you find from A to B in each one?

Be very careful—these diagrams are quite tricky.

  a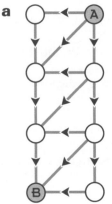

  b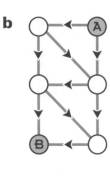

_____

_____

Fibonacci numbers

In the sequence, each term after the second is the sum of the two previous terms:

1, 1, 2, 3, 5, 8, 13, 21, 34, ...

1 Write down the next six terms of the sequence.

_____ , _____ , _____ , _____ , _____ , _____

The sequence of Fibonacci numbers occurs in nature. The spirals of sunflowers and pineapples and the petals of many flowers follow this pattern. Find some examples of these yourself.

The sequence has some fascinating properties.

2 **a** Add the first six terms, $1 + 1 + 2 + 3 + 5 + 8$, and compare this sum with the eighth term.

b Add the first seven terms, $1 + 1 + 2 + 3 + 5 + 8 + 13$, and compare this sum with the ninth term.

c Without adding, what do you think the sum of the first 10 terms will be?_____

3 Consider three consecutive Fibonacci numbers; for example:

a 3, 5, 8
$5^2 - 8 \times 3 = 25 - 24$
$= 1$

b 8, 13, 21
$13^2 - 8 \times 21 = 169 - 168$
$= 1$

c 13, 21, 34
$13 \times 34 - 21^2 = 442 - 441$
$= 1$

Notice how **c** differs from **a** and **b**. Try some examples yourself and express your findings in words.

4 Consider four consecutive Fibonacci numbers: 2, 3, 5, 8 or 3, 5, 8, 13.

Multiply the first and last numbers and compare the result with the product of the middle two. What do you notice?

5 Here are some interesting patterns. Complete the sums, and then write the next two lines for each set.

a
$$1^2 + 1^2 = 1 \times 2$$
$$1^2 + 1^2 + 2^2 = 2 \times 3$$
$$1^2 + 1^2 + 2^2 + 3^2 = 3 \times 5$$
$$1^2 + 1^2 + 2^2 + 3^2 + 5^2 = \text{_____}$$
$$1^2 + 1^2 + 2^2 + 3^2 + 5^2 + 8^2 = \text{_____}$$
_____
_____

b
$$1^3 + 2^3 - 1^3 = 8$$
$$2^3 + 3^3 - 1^3 = 34$$
$$3^3 + 5^3 - 2^3 = \text{_____}$$
_____
_____

6 Give some examples to show that the sum of any ten consecutive Fibonacci numbers is always divisible by 11.

$2 + 3 + 5 + 8 + 13 + 21 + 34 + 55 + 89 + 144 = 374$
$= 34 \times 11$

7 What type of numbers are these?

a every third in the sequence

b every fourth in the sequence

c every fifth in the sequence

d every sixth in the sequence

Repeating cycles

If you take the number 1, double it, double it again and then again and so continue doubling, you will get the sequence:

1, 2, 4, 8, 16, 32, 64, 128, 256, ...

If you now write down the end (unit) digits of this sequence, you will have:

1, 2, 4, 8, 6, 2, 4, 8, 6, ...

These unit digits form a pattern of repeating cycles:

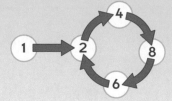

1　**a**　If you start with 3 and keep doubling, you will get the sequence:

3, 6, 12, 24, 48, 96, 192, 384, 768, ...

If you then write down the unit digits of this sequence, you will have:

3, 6, 2, 4, 8, 6, 2, 4, 8, ...

Draw the repeating cycle for this sequence.

b　Draw the repeating cycle of unit digits starting with 4, 5, 6, 7, 8, 9 and 10, repeating the doubling procedure.

2　**a**　If you start with 4 and write down the multiples of 4, you will get the sequence:

4, 8, 12, 16, 20, 24, 28, 32, 36, 40, 44, ...

Draw the repeating cycle for the unit digits of this sequence.

b　Show that the repeating cycle of unit digits with multiples of 7 is:

_____

_____

_____

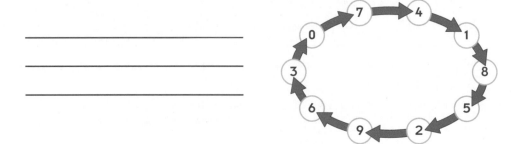

c　Investigate the repeating cycle of unit digits with multiples of 2, 3, 5, 6, 8 and 9.

Working Mathematically

Power cycling

You can use a calculator to carry out these investigations.

1 Start with 2 and consider the sequence of numbers obtained by successive multiplication by 2.

	2×1	2×2	$2 \times 2 \times 2$	$2 \times 2 \times 2 \times 2$	$2 \times 2 \times 2 \times 2 \times 2$	$2 \times 2 \times 2 \times 2 \times 2 \times 2$
Mathematical shorthand	2^1	2^2	2^3	2^4	2^5	2^6
Value	2	4	8	16	32	64
End (unit) digit	2	4	8	6	2	4

The unit digits form a pattern of repeating cycles.

Check to see whether 2^7 and 2^8 and others in the sequence fit the cycle pattern. Remember that in the expressions 2^3, 2^4 and 2^5 the superior (upper) numbers 3, 4 and 5 are known as powers.

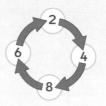

If you start with 5, consider a sequence of numbers obtained by successive multiplication by 5 and then write down the unit digits; you will obtain a *degenerate* cycle: there is only one number.

Here you see the unit digits of powers of 5.

5×1	5×5	$5 \times 5 \times 5$	$5 \times 5 \times 5 \times 5$	$5 \times 5 \times 5 \times 5 \times 5$
$5^1 = 5$	$5^2 = 25$	$5^3 = 125$	$5^4 = 625$	$5^5 = 3125$
↑	↑	↑	↑	↑

2 Investigate the patterns of unit digits of powers of 3, 4, 6, 7, 8 and 9. Draw the repeating cycles for each one.

3 By using the pattern of repeating cycles, work out the unit digits of:

a 2^2 _____

b 2^6 _____

c 2^{10} _____

d 2^{14} _____

e 2^4 _____

f 2^8 _____

g 2^{12} _____

h 2^{16} _____

i 3^2 _____

j 3^6 _____

k 3^{10} _____

l 3^{18} _____

m 7^3 _____

n 7^7 _____

o 7^{11} _____

p 7^{15} _____

q 9^4 _____

r 9^{12} _____

s 4^5 _____

t 4^7 _____

u 6^{11} _____

v 10^9 _____

w 11^{13} _____

x 11^{25} _____

In a canoe

Equipment: discs

1 Two girls and two boys go rowing in a canoe that can seat five people in a row. At first they sit (as illustrated) facing the centre, but then decide to change ends.

To avoid overturning the canoe, they must follow certain rules.

Each person:

• can slide to the next seat if it is empty;
• can slide past only one person before sitting down again;
• cannot jump or slide backwards.

Show that eight is the smallest number of moves required to completely reverse the positions of girls and boys.

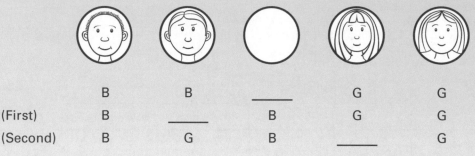

To experiment, cut out discs, draw a girl's head or a boy's head on each one and place them on circles. Indicate the moves you make like this:

	B	B	___	G	G
(First)	B	___	B	G	G
(Second)	B	G	B	___	G

2 This time three girls and three boys go rowing in a canoe that can seat seven people. The challenge is to find the smallest number of moves it will take to reverse the positions of girls and boys.

You will need two more discs (one for a boy and one for a girl) to experiment this time. _____

3 Try interchanging four girls and four boys in a nine-seat canoe. Use eight discs to work out your moves. (This is a difficult problem. Attempt it only if you had no trouble solving the other problems.) Find the smallest number of moves.

_____

4 Look for a pattern in your previous solutions, continue the pattern and try to predict the number of moves needed for five girls and five boys to change places.

Number of girls and boys	Number of moves
1	3
2	8
3	

Happy numbers

A calculator will be useful in this exercise.

Choose a two-digit number.
Square each of its digits and add the two squares.
Square the digits of the result and again add the squares.
Repeat the process.
Keep going until:

a   you reach 1; or

b   you find that the numbers are repeated in a cycle.

   If a sequence reaches 1, the original number is called HAPPY.

   If it does not, it is called SAD.

Here is an example:

23

Square:	2	3
Add squares:	4 + 9 = **13**
Square:	1 3
Add squares:	1 + 9 = **10**
Square:	1 0
Add squares:	1 + 0 = **1** **STOP! 23 is happy**

To investigate what happens to a one-digit number, such as 2, start squaring the digit
(2 → 4 → 16) and proceed as above.

You might find it easier to set out your work like this:

23 → 4 + 9 = 13 → 1 + 9 = 10 → 1 + 0 = 1

1   Since 23 is happy, what can you say about 32? _____

2   From the example above, what can you say about 13 and 10? _____

3   Which numbers between 2 and 50 are happy and which are sad? _____

4   Can you predict (with no working) which numbers will be happy and which sad?

_____

_____

_____

_____

_____

Note that numbers will form different styles of chains.

Some will form a closed loop: a short loop: or a long loop:

Mixed challenges

1 In a science lab there were some three-legged stools and some four-legged stools. There were 29 stools altogether and a total of 102 legs. How many three-legged stools were there in the lab? _____

2 In the last form elections at our school, 75 votes were cast. Candidate Popular received twice as many votes as candidate Helpful. Candidate Jolly had nine more than candidate Sporty and six more than Helpful. Jolly won ten times as many votes as candidate Bossy.

How many votes did each candidate receive?

Jolly	Bossy	Sporty	Popular	Helpful

3 Greedygrimes Charley ate a total of 100 jelly beans in five days, each day eating six more than on the previous day.

How many jelly beans did he eat on the third day? _____

Day	1	2	3	4	5
Jelly beans eaten					

4 Suppose K, L and M represent the scores in the three regions of a dartboard. The sum of K and L is 7, the sum of L and M is 17 and the sum of K and M is 14. What are the values of K, L and M?

K _____   L _____   M _____

5 **a** In a mathematics competition there are 15 problems. For every correct answer you are awarded three marks, but if an answer is incorrect one mark is deducted from the score.

If Carl attempted all 15 questions and his score was 29, how many did he answer correctly? _____

Answers		Total score
Correct (3 marks)	(Incorrect (–1 mark)	

b In another maths competition, you are awarded five marks for each question answered correctly and one mark is deducted for an incorrect answer.

If there are 30 questions in the competition, and a student who attempts all 30 receives 108 marks, how many of the student's answers were wrong?

_____

Working Mathematically

Logic puzzles

Equipment: matches

Think about these questions very carefully.

1 If it takes 5 minutes to make one cut, how long will it take to cut a 7 metre pole into ten equal pieces? _____

2 Robert has a 10 cm × 10 cm × 10 cm block of cheese. What is the smallest number of cuts that will divide the block into 2 cm cubes? _____

3 An express train travelling at 80 km/h leaves Sydney for Canberra at the same time as a slow train leaves Canberra for Sydney travelling at 35 km/h.

Which train will be further from Sydney when they meet? _____

4 A certain substance doubles its volume every minute. At 9:00 a.m. a small amount is placed in a container, and at exactly 10:00 a.m. the container is full. Work out the time at which the container was:

a half full; _____

b one-quarter full. _____

5 Arrange nine matches together to form five triangles.

6 Arrange six matches to form four equilateral (equal-sided) triangles. (You must not break any match.)

7 Draw four straight lines so that you move through all nine dots in this diagram without lifting your pencil from the paper or tracing over any line already drawn.

- • •
- • •
- • •

8 Scout leader Jim wants to place four flags so that each one is the same distance from the other three.

How can he do this? Make a model, using matches, and measure the distances.

9 Can you remove two matches from this figure so that only two squares will remain?

10 One of nine valuable coins is slightly heavier than the rest, although all are identical in appearance. Using a balance scale, how can the heavier coin be identified by using the scale only twice?

Models or diagrams

1 A log is cut into four pieces in 12 minutes.
At this rate, how long will it take to cut a log into six pieces? _____

2 The lengths of three rods are 7 cm, 9 cm and 15 cm.
There are no measurements marked on them, but
we can measure a 2 cm length by placing two of
them side by side, as can be seen in the illustration.

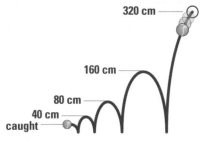

Draw clear diagrams to show how you can use the
three rods to measure lengths of:

a 6 cm   **b** 16 cm   **c** 1 cm   **d** 24 cm

e 17 cm   **f** 22 cm   **g** 13 cm.

3 A ball is dropped from a height of 320 cm.
At each bounce it comes up to half the height from
which it fell. If it is caught at the top point of a
bounce of 20 cm, what distance
has the ball travelled altogether? _____

Study the illustration carefully before you
answer the question.

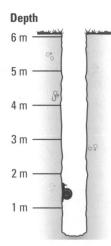

4 Two snails were climbing out of a hole 6 metres deep.

a In each hour, the first snail spent the first
30 minutes climbing up 3 metres and the last
30 minutes sliding back 1 metre, while it rested.

How long did it take this
snail to reach the top? _____

b The second snail could only manage to climb
2 metres in 30 minutes, and in the next
30 minutes it also slid back 1 metre.

How long did it take this
snail to reach the top? _____

5 Riva and Lee decide to go rowing on the river to a spot 10 km away. They row
4 km in 30 minutes, then rest in the rowboat for 10 minutes during which time
the current drags them back 1 km. This pattern is repeated until they reach their
destination. Calculate how long it will take the girls to reach:

a a point 7 km from where they started; _____

b their destination. _____

Working Mathematically